Little Weena's Flowers

Little Weena's Flowers

Louva A. Hunt

Dedication

For my parents, whose gift of love for each other, their family
and fellow man pays forward through all time.

Contents

Acknowledgments

First credits go to my children, each of whom has contributed uniquely to this work – legal research, expertise in firearms history, literary critique and editing, transport to research sites and in general as team members of a dedicated cheering squad. I give special thanks to my daughter Nita, for her work with the illustrations, research and preparation of the manuscript.

To my coworker, Charles Lyles, for the illustrations he contributed to this work and for his compassionate work with so many traumatized young people. His sketching pencil can find the soul of a human within a prison mug shot.

Special thanks to Broadus Spivey for his critique and advice. His wife Ruth Ann, and her twin Rebecca Chudacoff, were special cast members in the story and generously contributed to the editing and research.

I salute Roger Estlack, one link in a chain of Estlacks who have always been on the scene reporting Clarendon news. I am grateful for his contribution to this work and for his contributions to the stewardship of the priceless historic collection of those newspapers.

I stand in awe of the age of digital research, without which this untold story would never have been found. To all of the librarians, archivist and historical societies who opened their collections and websites to me, thanks. Among these, special credits go to Jean Stavenhagen of the Donley County Historical Commission. She kept me resourced and on task. I pay respect to those archivists who, out of a sense of responsibility for disclosure, denied my requests. They redirected my writing toward the far more accurate verification of historic perspective.

And, the ultimate gratitude goes to an unspoken prayer directed to the newspaper on the kitchen table.

To one and all, a special flower from Little Weena.

Little Weena's Flowers

H. G WELLS' Time Traveler arrived to the year 802,701 AD aboard
his Time Machine and viewed with dismay what he thought to be
the wane of humanity. Amid the apathy and complacency of that race
he watched a helpless little creature being swept away in the currents of
a great river.

"What if cruelty had grown into a common passion? What if in this
interval the race had lost its manliness, and had developed into something inhuman, unsympathetic, and overwhelmingly powerful?"

In an act of compassion, The Time Traveler reached out to save the
creature, Little Weena. During the rest of his sojourn into the future
she danced at his side stuffing exotic white flowers into his pockets and
covering his hands with kisses of gratitude and tenderness.[1]

Louva Hunt, 1938, taken by Ernest L. Hunt

1

The Buttercup Years

DUST DEVILS HAPPEN when starkly different forces suddenly come together in the same space. Warm air rises from the earth into a pool of cool air drifting by and starts the spin. Wisps of the rising funnel reach out and dance about gathering stray particles into the swirl. As the inert particles collide they become the debris that electrically charge the momentum of the twister for a brief time before the energy dissipates, and the willy-willy of stray bits scatter unnoticed to the earth. Dust devils also dance over the landscape of Mars. When viewed from a distance, they leave behind spiderlike trails that cross the planet's surface and endure throughout time.

It was like that in my life in 1938. I was in a haven, the eye of an idyllic eddy, unaware of the torments in the world that were about to swirl about it. And even as the swirl was forming I noticed the particles as they rushed by but not the whirlwind driving them. On our 20 acre farm outside the eastern edge of Clarendon, Texas, It was the spring that the stack lot erupted with a solid cover of buttercups, yellow in the center and pink at the edge of the petals. A big hay stack was positioned at the west edge of the lot leaving the rest for the buttercups and freedom for the wind to ripple through them. I used the haystack as my easy chair for resting in the shade and sucking sweet juice from pulp of feed cane stalks stolen from within the stack. This was kept a secret because my parents had warned that chewing into the tough green bark of the cane would wear my teeth off to the gums. I devised a way of twisting a joint of the cane until the bark split and I could extract the juice through the slats. There was a hazard involved in that scheme. The edges of the slats were sharp and they sometimes clamped shut on a piece of my tongue. But my teeth were not worn away.

With the hay stack between me and the house, I had a private world. I could zoom in on things like the one lone buttercup growing out of the center of a rusty coil of barbed wire lying at the corner of the fence and wonder how that flower had made its way out of the blow sand that almost covered the coil. That question was never answered because one day the buttercup was gone. The wire coil had been snatched up without regard for the flower and called into service to repair a hole in the fence where the milk cow had broken into our neighbor's cotton patch. What was left of the blow sand quickly melted away in the spring showers and even I forgot the buttercup.

One morning in the fall after the buttercups had gone to seed and the stack lot field had turned brown I answered a knock on our front door. As I opened the door a small black man stepped back holding his hat in both hands over his chest and bowed so that I could not see his face.

"Yore mama at home?" he asked. Mother called back from the kitchen saying she was coming. I opened the screen door as an invitation for him to come in the house. He quickly stepped even further back away from the door and made even deeper bowing motions. When Mother arrived she pointed toward the barn and gave him some brief instructions. He responded with more bows and left in the direction of the barn replacing his hat and walking upright.

"Why did he stand that way?" I asked my mother.

"What way?"

I mimicked the bowing and hat holding.

Mother smiled. "Oh, he does not want to frighten you. He was just being polite. He is Ham, Ham McCampbell, the butcher.[2] He is here to kill our hog. You'll have to stay in the house out of his way while he is working."

What I saw peeping out of the back kitchen window at the hog killing did not match the romantic stories about hog killing I had heard the adults tell. What they talked about sounded more like a picnic where neighbors gathered to build a fire for scalding and fried sausage and rubbed salt onto hams.[3] What I saw was Ham at his wagon erecting a tall black triangle behind the windmill water tank. I could see smoke curling out of a fire under a large black pot of steaming hot water and fragmentary glimpses of him moving in and out of my view of the pot. Later that day he approached the back door and handed buckets of raw meat to my mother. He talked to her there, sometimes without the stepping back and bowing. Once he smiled and showed me his face. Only now can I see how the hog killing day entered the space of an earlier day in the summer – the day I caught the wild kitten.

That spring a stray cat in family way had found shelter under our house and nested her five grey stripped kittens in sight but just out of reach behind the corner post that anchored the house a foot or so off of the ground. That created the adventure for me - to catch one of the kittens. The quest had endured for weeks with nothing to show for my efforts but a lot of scratches on my arms and some ominous itchy bumps under my hopelessly tangled hair. One hot August day I finally made the capture. Dressed in my blue denim overalls with bits of Bermuda grass clinging to the fresh blood oozing from my arms I was clenching the kitten when my mother called to me from the back door. She was telling me that I had to come in the house and take a bath because we were going to town.

About then my father came to the door holding his new camera. That had been his adventure, to finally own the Graflex camera he had been admiring in the Photography Magazine. His challenge was to launch a career as a free-lance photojournalist and I was his first model.

"Let me get a picture first," he said. I sat on the cellar door and squeezed the cat to prevent his escape. Daddy snapped the picture and my parents smiled at each other. I heard Daddy say, "She has no idea how her life is about to change." They seemed happy with what they envisioned was ahead for me. I was not at all certain that I was. None of us could imagine what actually lay ahead.

I took an extra hard scrubbing for that bath from a course washrag vigorously rubbed over a bar of Ivory. Watching the soap bar float in the bath water diverted my resistance to the scrubbing. The tangles were relentlessly combed from my hair and my scab covered knees and cat scratched arms were coated with ample dabs of Jergen's beauty lotion. All of this was to ready me for a meeting in the basement of the Presbyterian Church with a lady I would later know as Mrs. George Bagby, the casting director for the Tom Thumb Wedding.

I held onto my mother's hands as we went down the stairs to the door surrounded by a small box-like entrance made of concrete walls. It smelled like moist concrete as basements do. Inside Mrs. Bagby invited us to sit in a straight chair beside her desk. She rustled through a stack of papers with lists of names punctuated with edit in and out scratches and she looked me over. I was certain she had noticed the cat scratches. I tried to cover them with my hands.

"We don't have a partner yet for Jimmy Frank Heath. He is Franklin Roosevelt." She checked for my mother's response. "That means she would be Eleanor?"

My mother nodded and Mrs. Bagby quickly returned the stack of papers to her desk. They continued talking about other things. I was thinking about the problem with being Eleanor Roosevelt. I sensed from the way she asked the question that there might be something wrong with it, but that worry did not last long. We were quickly on our way to get a good parking spot along Main Street for Saturday night in Clarendon.

Those Saturday nights in Clarendon when the county folk came to town to shop, to bring the cream and eggs they would trade for groceries or simply to go from car to car visiting with friends. Mother liked getting to town early so she could park in front of Greene Dry Goods store where she would be at the center of the gathering of her friends. I was in the back seat of our car waiting for it to be time for my weekly visit to the picture show. I saw a black boy, eight or nine, walking down the sidewalk of Main Street. He stopped to admire the display of watches and jewelry in the Goldston display window located in that corner of the drugstore building. I always stopped at that display window too. It was a favorite among the list of treats I enjoyed during the Saturday rituals. But suddenly the black boy was scolded by one of the old men sitting on the "spit and whittle bench" in front of Greene Dry Goods [4] and ordered him to get off of the sidewalk. The old man was angry and when the boy ignored his order he pushed him to the gutter beneath the edge of the sidewalk.

"Boy, you need to learn your place. You don't walk on our sidewalks. You walk down there in the gutter where you belong." He waved his arms angrily and a cluster of other men began to gather around him in support.

On his way from the gutter into the street the boy passed by my family's car. His face was only inches from mine as his body brushed against the outside of the car. He looked down at his scuff toed shoes and the gutter. Unformed tears lined his eyelids; hurt and shame was there and a tension in his jaw as he quickened his pace up the street past the Pastime movie theater, not back across the tracks. I saw the anger he was reserving for another time. Seeing how awkwardly he walked in the ill fitted hand-me-down clothes caused me to squirm uncomfortably in my seat. I felt as though I had been the one receiving the scolding. The trousers were baggy and too big for him. The shoes that he wore without socks had once belonged to an adult and they slipped on his heel. At that time I actually sensed the dust devil swirl – dizzy and confused - though I decided to think about the Lone Ranger movie instead and whether I would buy popcorn or an Almond Joy to go with it.

In weeks that followed I started to school and as if that was not enough, plans for the Tom Thumb Wedding were gearing up. I started thinking again about Eleanor Roosevelt and what that name meant. I overheard some jokes about her being ugly but the way my parents coached me for the role made me feel that she was a lady they admired. My father taught me to quote things, in her eastern accent, that she said in speeches. He invited me to listen to The March of Time broadcast and imitate her as they did. My mother told me that the lady loved the color blue and that a certain shade of it had been named for her. She would fashion an elegant evening gown for me of blue satin, Eleanor Blue. From blue denim to blue satin began to appeal to me. All that Ivory soap and Jergen's lotion was the adjustment.

One of the next things to happen was my maiden voyage to White and Kirk's in Amarillo where the entire fourth floor of that high fashion clothing store was devoted to fabrics for hand tailored clothing. The selection of the fabric for the gown was to take place in this impressive setting. I was chin level with the long counters where the clerks rolled out the riches from rectangular bolts or the even more impressive long spools. I had to reach up to finger the long sheets of fabric being examined by my mother. She squeezed them in her hand to test for how they wrinkled. She pulled each one diagonally between outstretched arms to see how it was on the bias. She examined the weave on the reverse side. As the seamstress she narrowed the selection. As the model I made the final decision of which shining blue fabric I wanted for my evening gown. My education continued as I watched the clerk hold strands of thread against the fabric to match for color and lengths of lace at the edge to satisfy the tastes of my mother.

That venture had been the fun part. I protested having to stand still for the fittings of the gown. Mother stroked and adjusted the satin pieces and pinned them into place. The sewing pins pricked my shoulders and waist. The rehearsals were not all that much fun either. Those meant assembling 48 make believe dignitaries with that many mothers in the College auditorium and having them wait their turn to walk down the aisle to take a designated spot on the stage. Add in the individual instructions from the several directors on how to play the parts from the Duke and Duchess of Windsor to the Prime Minister of England to, of course, Franklin Delano and Eleanor Roosevelt.

Dress rehearsal had been that Sunday afternoon. For the first time I had felt gentle caresses of the satin on my newly scrubbed and creamed skin. My escort, Jimmy Frank Heath, managed well to keep the monocle in his eye socket, make proper gestures with his cane and keep his arm positioned to support my hand escorting me through the evening as any gentlemanly President would. All things were going as planned for months now. The only surprise was the Spring-like rain shower that sent some of the mothers running outside to roll up car windows. I watched with fascination as some man closed the tandem windows next to the tall ceiling of the auditorium with a black tool long enough to reach that high. The rain was over by the time he was done and as we left the rehearsal was forgotten except that the fall air smelled clean and the earth was moist.

Back home it was a routine Sunday evening. We rushed through supper and getting ready for bed so we could gather around the Zenith radio in the living room to hear our favorite, Charlie McCarthy. At 8:00 p.m. the program ended.[5] With my Eleanor gown hanging in the closet behind my bed, ready for the real performance next Thursday night, I snuggled into my bed ready to sleep and dream about being an elegant lady.

Just as I was sinking into the haziness of sleep, the windmill outside the bedroom window groaned when a sudden gust of wind rushed toward the blades and they pivoted to receive it. The gears squeaked and with a click and clang sent the sucker rod descending into the depth for its harvest. The wind whirl climaxed to a velocity that slapped the rod against the sides of the casing pipe with a fury, and then as quickly as it had arrived, the wind died, the mill grew still and again silence joined the greyness of that night and I slept.

Sometime later in the night the silence was interrupted by a man's voice calling to my father through the window. The voice was a familiar one and it was not alarming but the words it spoke frightened me. I awoke to another world.

"Ernest, this is Guy Wright, get your gun. Something bad has happened over by colored town; the sheriff is calling out the American Legion to form a posse."

"What happened?" replied my father from his bed.

"I can't say it. . . . Come out here and I'll tell you."

They met outside in the yard only a few feet from my bed. I could hear them talking in whispered tones but could not distinguish their words. Guy Wright was a long- time friend of the family so his voice was familiar and not alarming to me, but the words of his message sent my mind to racing. "Posse" was not my image of the American Legion. These were friends of my father who wore khaki green caps and marched with their guns and carried flags in the Fourth of July parade. Others of these men stood together in front of the Pastime theater and snapped to attention to salute the colors as they passed by. I associated "posse" with scenes from Western movies – hordes of men mounted on galloping horses firing their six shooters in the air as they ran down some desperado.

When Daddy was back inside the house he motioned for Mother to come with him to the small hallway between the bathroom door and the door to the closet behind my bed. This was the spot they often chose to talk about things they wished to conceal from my brother and I. He shared their bedroom so this maneuver worked for him. I had learned to lay still, feigning sleep, and listen. It became my favorite window to the adult world.

In grim tones my father defined the desperado to my mother, choosing the words allowed for use with women and children. "Some Negro has attacked two white women near the dump ground and he is still on the loose. Guy Pierce, the sheriff, is deputizing the American Legion to form a manhunt. We are to meet at Walter Green's place."

The closet where the blue gown hung also served as the place where my father stored his guns and ammunition. I heard ominous noises. He took out his 30-40 Krag and carried it through the clicking and clinking procedures of loading that gun.[6] As the most powerful and prized of his collection of guns, this process had always been executed out of my sight. So that my brother or I might not learn by seeing how it was loaded, this was one of his safety procedures. I had learned to identify the loading by sound. The process had a distinct rhythm, like a tapping out prelude to a drum drill. Next, I heard the 410 shotgun clicked open and loaded. I was familiar with that process.

He came out of the closet with a long barreled revolver, unloaded, for my mother to be shown how to cock the hammer and squeeze the trigger. I watched her thumb straining to reach up for the hammer and her face flinch when the trigger snapped. I strained my own thumbs in chorus. After several snaps he nodded his approval and took the gun and opened out the gate to the cylinder and began loading it. Nestled against my mother's thigh my eyes were in line with the cylinder as he turned it into place and pushed a cartridge into each chamber. I watched as he spun the loaded cylinder and snapped the gate back into place.

I was familiar with these guns. I had been invited to tag along with my father on coyote hunting and target practice trips and watched him perform these rituals of checking and loading. Along with my mother and brother I had been schooled personally in the use of the 410 shotgun. We were routinely given gun safety lessons emphasizing the power and danger of carelessness with guns. We were guided through target practice sessions carefully using the safety practices. My parents told me I was a good shot. My father lovingly assured my mother that she was a good shot too by calling her his Annie Oakley. But until that night being a good shot meant nothing more than shooting rabbits or bottles and tin cans. Tonight my mind had to grapple with the idea of using the guns for a manhunt.

My father locked the front door and the outside door to their bed-room and for the back door with no lock, he showed Mother how to secure it by propping the back of the cane bottomed chair in under the doorknob and holding it shut by sitting in the chair. As I listened to Daddy give her the orders on what she was to do, I felt distanced from the scene as though I was watching a movie with my parents playing a role no more real than me being Eleanor Roosevelt. My father was tell-ing my mother how to kill a man and she was calmly listening as though she intended to carry out the orders.

"Don't let anyone come close to the house unless he can identify himself. If any of the posse men come here to check, they will tell you who they are. If anyone else comes toward the house and won't identify himself, use this first."

He leaned the 410 against the door loaded and ready to fire. I re-membered having held that gun in my hands and looking down the barrel at my target, a bottle or old tin can, and watching it disintegrate when I squeezed the trigger.

"If that doesn't stop him, use this as a last resort." He laid the Colt 45 across her lap.

That gun was like the six shooters in the movies. The picture in my mind of it was the memory of seeing a rabbit as its target and later hav-ing to watch my father and brother pull the skin off of what was left of the rabbit. That sent me scrambling back under my covers. I listened as Daddy left with his gun and drove down the lane by our house to his mission. For me what followed was a long and frightening night. [7] The horrors I imaged were of men I knew roaming the countryside in the night with their own guns in pursuit of a man who attacked women, of an invader that might break into the range of my mother's guns. I worried about my daddy being in colored town. This was a place sepa-rated from my world by some kind of barrier that formed along the rail-road tracks. I commonly heard the rules that kept the barrier in place. "Good Negroes knew their place" and that was north of the tracks in a place called colored town. That was especially true after dark when "no Negro would be found south of the tracks." Before now I had never thought about how that sorting was done.

I endured the dark silence of that night with my self-appointed mission of listening for unusual sounds and to assure that my mother did not sleep on her watch. Peeping out from under the covers I had gathered over my head I awoke often and if her eyes had closed I made some sound that popped them back open again.

We did not have a watch dog. That was the reason we had the 410 shotgun in the first place. In those Depression days when people were hungry, dogs were hungry too. They would eat the chicken feed that sustained my mother's chicken flock - our meat and eggs. Town dogs, individually someone's docile pet, formed packs with others to raid our chicken feeder and sometimes the chickens themselves. So, Daddy got the 410 and taught her how to "pepper" the marauding dogs with birdshot and send them yelping back to town. During the times that I dozed that night memories of those scenes reassured me. Sometime before dawn the silence was broken by the sound of my father's voice calling out his name:

"Maggie, its Ernest. I'm home." He repeated this several times before he reached the back door. Still holding the .45 she pulled the chair away and opened the door for him. They faced each other smiling, but still vigilant, they did not embrace. At the closet behind my bed they talked as he unloaded and put the guns away. He described how the Legionnaires had been lined up in the country lane near where the attack occurred and sworn in as Deputies by the Sheriff. They had been sent out in teams of two and three to block all roads leading from town and to search colored town house by house.

"They caught him. The Texas Rangers already have him in Amarillo for safe keeping. They dismissed us."

"The Rangers caught him?"

"They have him now. Actually it was Clyde Douglas who tracked him down. He picked up his tracks at the scene and followed them into town. Another team had checked that shanty at first and thought it was suspicious about the way two of the men were acting. They seemed to be nervous about a third man who was asleep there. The tracks that Clyde had found led to the same shanty. The posse men went back a third time and decided to call in the sheriff. They found the shoes under the bed and matched them to the tracks Clyde found. That was enough to arrest him and turn him over to the Rangers. He isn't one of our local Negroes; he's visiting from up North somewhere, Chicago, I think."

Clyde James Douglas, (1891-1982) Pharmacist and World War I veteran tracked Morris Norman to the shanty where he slept.

It was like a Western movie to me. All had ended well. I relaxed and went back to sleep. I awoke at daybreak to resume my little girl life at school. The annual school Halloween Carnival would be tonight and my upcoming debut as Eleanor would happen this Thursday. Nothing about those things was any different. I didn't hear anyone talking about the Negro either. Not until the day after the *Tom Thumb Wedding*. The wedding came off as it had been rehearsed so many times. It gave me memories of wearing the gown for the whole evening and seeing Daddy flashing pictures of everyone with his new camera.

In those days we received our papers by mail, which meant that Daddy brought them home at night from our mailbox in the Post Office. They were discussed at the breakfast table the next morning. In the case of the Clarendon papers there was always some manipulation of datelines because they came out on Thursdays only. Some news was reported and other news was predicted. That Friday morning after the *Tom Thumb Wedding* I studied my father's face as he held the paper and talked to my mother about "swift justice" and "within the law." I had never seen his face look exactly that way before. It was somewhere between when he was correcting me for some misbehavior and the way he looked when he saluted the Flag in the Fourth of July parade.

He noticed my concern and changed the subject by pointing to headlines at the other corner of the paper with a smile.

"RULERS OF THE HOME TO PRESENT THEIR ROYAL TOM THUMB WEDDING: Forty-seven Characters Included in Cast of Play at College Auditorium Beginning at 7:30 this Evening." With pride he read it aloud. His finger skipped on down to the paragraph beginning with "Guests: Duke of Windsor, Bobby Brown: his Duchess, Layma V. Tatum. Franklin Delano Roosevelt, Jimmie Frank Heath. Duke of Kent, John Miller Morris: his Duchess, Sarah Rains." Another look crossed his face. [8] He stopped reading aloud and silently scanned the article over and over. Mother took the paper from him and read it for herself.

"They left her name out. The only one they didn't mention. After all that . . ." Daddy motioned for her to be quiet.

"We know she was there. I have a lot of pictures to prove it. I'll get those developed tonight and we can show everyone how pretty a lady Miss Eleanor Roosevelt was."

Jimmy Frank Heath and Louva Hunt as Franklin Delano and Eleanor Roosevelt. Photo by Ernest L. Hunt, November 3, 1938.

"Send one to the paper," mother snapped.

Daddy smiled. "More people saw her there than read the paper." He put the paper away and readied me to leave for school with him. For him I pretended that it didn't matter. *But it did.*

That weekend we were brought back to the topic of the Negro and the manhunt by my mother's barrage of questions about it. She wanted to see the scene of the crime and the shanty where they caught the assailant. Daddy explained to her the reason the Sheriff had wanted to seal colored town off for safety reasons. He reminded her that the Legionnaires had been sworn to honor and implement that request before they were dismissed. "We have a duty to keep the peace - law and order." He said those words in a stern voice. My parents finally worked out a compromise. "This weekend, I'll take you to the dump ground where it happened. We can go in the back way."

The dump ground was less than a mile from our house. If we drove the narrow back lane that weaved west through the blow sand dunes north of the railroad tracks at the shipping pen crossing, we could get there without having to drive through colored town. I knew that route and the dump grounds. We had made trips there, not to leave the unburnable refuse it was set aside for, but to leave carefully packed boxes of hand-me-down clothing and discarded house wares at the edge of the dump. Those that brought their discarded items there reasoned that the Negro families who needed these things could sort through the garbage and find them. I felt ashamed of this kind of faceless charity. I preferred to think about things I could do if I really were Eleanor Roosevelt. I would give every colored child a birthday party and give him gift wrapped boxes of new clothes. On top of every box there would be a watch or a ring from Goldston's jewelry store.

On Saturday Daddy kept his promise. As our car reached the edge of the dump I imagined seeing the face of the black boy in front of Goldston's on a number of black children bending down to rummage through boxes. My fingers remembered reaching up to feel sheets of silk and satin and the sensations of wearing rings that had been rewards at birthdays and Christmas of my enjoyment of Goldston's window displays. As I look back, there may have been some type casting to my role as Eleanor. I had strong feelings about things not being the same for me and for those who had to walk in the gutter and find their shoes in discarded boxes.

The scene of the crime was at a corner that turned west past the dump ground one block from where the lane turned north from colored town toward the garden farm home of the victims. Dust Bowl blow sand had piled up to the top of the four wire corner post and also covered most of the north rut and bar ditch of the lane. Daddy was answering Mother's question about the crime and the capture.

"This sand was damp enough that night to hold a good track. It even held the skid marks where he dragged her into the bushes. He was wearing a type of shoe they must wear up North with a heel that left a distinct cross in the sand. Clyde picked that up with his flashlight. Part of the time he got down on his hands and knees but he followed it right up to the front path of that shanty. It's not too far from here." He nodded down the lane.

Mother moved in that direction hoping to see the shanty. A motion of his arm restrained her. "We all have a duty," he warned. She noticed that look in his face too. It started that night he left the house with his gun. We were supposed to obey that look.

I looked up the road where the silos were to the turnoff to Mrs. Jones' house. I loved going with Mother to buy vegetables from Mrs. Jones. We had never been to the house because Mrs. Jones always met us outside and talked to us through the passenger side car window where I was sitting. The loud words of Mother's order brushed over me. Always smiling and nodding but saying little, Mrs. Jones scurried off toward her barn with the order in her mind. She returned with baskets of vegetables and mother gave her money. I especially liked the Spring trips there to buy garden bedding plants because the long, long lane from the road with the silos up to her house was lined with Locust trees and they were covered with clusters of white flowers that hung from the trees like grapes. They filled the air with a fragrance sweeter than Honeysuckle vines. I shuddered as I heard my father tell my mother about how the Negro had beaten Mrs. Jones on the head with a rock until she fell to the ground. I looked about the dump ground for something else to think about.

Something green caught my eye. It was a kitchen stove the same as my mother's stove except the oven that was built to sit upon the metal Queen Anne legs was a bright green and white porcelain instead of the dull black metal of mother's stove. The legs under the burner side of the green stove were missing. This tilt made the oven rise up into the beams of sunlight that broke through clumps of trees lining the dump ground. In my mind I rearranged things so that this oven sat upon the legs of my mother's stove and caught the sunbeams that filtered through the green ruffled organza curtains at her kitchen window. I created an imaginary birthday party at the kitchen table with a round angel food cake frosted with sugary white merengue and decorated with those pink and green candy roses you peeled off a waxed paper card. In mother's treasured green Depression glass dessert dishes was homemade lime sherbet topped with a red Maraschino cherry. The sound of my mother's voice broke into my fantasy.

She was pressing my father for more details of things he was holding back from her. "What did the paper mean by 'lurid'?" [9]

With his back to me he faced my mother and feigned a motion that resembled picking up a person and slamming them upon the bank of blow sand. He spoke softly. I heard the words, "in her mouth" before a look of horror crossed my mother's face. It frightened me more than the sight of her sitting in the cane bottom chair with a gun across her lap. She paled and cupped her hands to her mouth. My father's hand gently stroked her shoulders as she bent over and heaved into the sandy ruts of the road. After that was over he took the white linen handkerchief he always carried in his hip pocket and dabbed her face with it and guided her back to the car with his arm around her waist. As we drove off toward home the sun dropped behind the clump of trees and cast a dark shadow over the green stove kneeling in the rubbish.

My parents had more of those serious discussions of the newspaper during breakfast. I heard more new words, "revolting attack," "mob violence," "jury trial." Daddy's face had that new duty look and Mother listened quietly more often than she talked.

One morning before Christmas Daddy looked at the paper silently. The duty look blended with a strange look of sadness. "Six weeks, from arrest to execution, six weeks." There was a tone of victory in his voice but as he laid the paper out on the table another look crossed his face and he bowed his head. It looked as though he was saying a prayer to the newspaper.[10]

I understood six weeks. That was the time between report cards. My life played out between those signal points. Soon time went beyond. We moved to town and I lost my haystack retreat. Outside play was in our yard and it was public with cars driving by and people watching. The excitement over Charley McCarthy with his shiny black shoes gave way to thrills over Dorothy's radiant red slippers skipping down the yellow brick path. Those six weeks were replaced in my memory with the things that were happening in a new world, one that was emerging from The Great Depression but facing into something worse. What returned from time to time was the picture of my daddy's bowed head over the paper and what never left me was my puzzlement about what that had meant.

2

The Time Machine

Forty years later, October 30, 1978, I was starting my day as usual with a cup of coffee and the morning paper. Atop the front page of the *Amarillo Daily News* was a feature article entitled, "October 30 memorable night in '38." It recalled that it was the night that Orson Welles sent much of the nation into panic with his radio dramatization of a Martian invasion.

> A MILLION IMAGINATIONS AFIRE AS RADIO
> REALISM SHAKES NATION. [1]

I skimmed the article and agreed with its focus – people in the Panhandle had not made much of the broadcast. I followed my usual ritual with the newspaper - skim the headlines first and read for details later. On that day a skim of the headlines noted that there were peace talks between Israel and Egypt, the Piltdown man was being called a hoax, experts were still testing for the authenticity of the Holy Shroud of Turin and the spaceship Voyager I was broadcasting remarkable pictures from outer space back to earth. [2] "Nothing new under the sun," I quoted to myself from Ecclesiastes. [3] I was ready to dismiss the paper as nothing new when a challenging thought caused me to pause.

If the *"War of the Worlds"* meant so little to people in the Panhandle why are we still hearing about it 40 years later? How did the *Amarillo Daily News* reporter pick up on the anniversary if he had not read it on some list of historic events? Then what was so historic about it? Through the years I had dismissed any mention of it as irrelevant, just something else Orson Welles had done to call attention to himself and to improve the profit margin of the faltering radio broadcast industry. Obviously he had succeeded. But it was success purchased with questionable tactics. First of all the creative source of the idea had belonged to H. G. Wells who published his story *"War of the Worlds"* in 1898. With either coincidental or contrived play on the surnames and the reputation of H. G. Wells to create suggestions of things to come Orson Welles' "radio realism" found fertile soil in the social anxieties of the populace. [4]

On the East Coast people readily believed illusions of 30 yard wide cylinders hissing and emitting snake-like creatures from Mars onto the landscape of earth. In the Panhandle people's curiosities were more realistic. Calls to the local radio and newspaper made inquiries about meteors, other natural disasters or German war attacks. And in the Panhandle these calls were limited to those who owned radios big enough to have picked up the East Coast broadcast. In 1938 those in the Panhandle who owned radios at all were limited. Newly appointed Director of the Texas Department of Public Safety, Homer Garrison, reported that his department had received no calls at all. At that a third reread of the article something seized my attention:

"There were personal horrors, though . . . as in the case of two Donley County women who were raped on their way home from church." [5]

With that I realized that I had been a part of that night. It was the night I had watched my father load his guns and leave my mother sitting in the cane bottom chair with one of them in her lap. Unbelievable. By now I had serious ambitions of becoming a writer and this news excited me. It was a story to write. Within days I was in the archives of the Panhandle Plains Museum searching for copies of the 1938 newspapers that covered the events. After a day there wrestling with spools of microfilm and the cumbersome film reader I returned home with a stack of overlapping copies of the 1938 papers. Like a jigsaw puzzle I pieced together paper sections of the November 3rd edition of the *Donley County Leader* to complete the headline:

"NEGRO CHARGED WITH ASSAULT WILL COME TO TRIAL TUESDAY: SPECIAL OFFICERS ARE DETAILED TO INSURE FAIR, SPEEDY TRIAL

Morris Norman, 20 year old smug, pretentious, Illinois Negro in jail cell in Amarillo, is today awaiting the outcome of an indictment charging him with criminal assault of a Clarendon white woman here last Sunday night." [6]

With the front page reconstructed, I saw that on the left hand side of it was the article announcing the performance of the *Royal Tom Thumb Wedding* that night. On the right side was the news article about the rape. There was no mention of Orson Welles. An amazing coincidence, those three things all happened on the same night and I never before made the connection. Curiously, I read about the *Tom Thumb Wedding.* Still fascinating was the idea that an entire community of parents, teachers, businessmen could be so caught up in the fantasy that world leaders and dignitaries could joyfully assemble for the fairytale wedding of a child princess and her prince charming. [7]

My first experience of that fairyland was on dress rehearsal night, the fateful night. I relived the first sensation of being Eleanor Roosevelt clothed in shining blue satin at the arm of the president. Hopeful that by now someone had noticed me on performance night, I read through the list of names of those who attended the wedding searching for my name. Of course it was still missing and surprisingly, that still mattered.

I returned to the right side of the paper. It was a night in history when the innocence of fantasy had collided in a brutal and shocking way with reality. For the rest of the country it was fear of invasions from space, for the citizens of Clarendon it was the intrusion of evil into the illusion of its Saint's Roost image. For me it was the first experience with a real threat of danger. As I observed my parents become a part of the community's response I felt reassured that we were being kept safe. My innocence survived that fateful night. I had been oblivious to the reality that the threats to my community had involved far more than the violence of one man.

But by 1978 such innocence had been shattered. By then I had lived through global wars in which men killed each other in mass. On April 4, 1968, I was in Detroit standing in the ruins, still smoldering with the hate and resentment left by 1967 mob violence, and that same night, having returned to Texas, watched TV as it reignited with the news of the assassination of Martin Luther King. Four months later I had been caught up in crowds of protesters for peace at the 1968 Democratic Convention in Chicago and watched them became mobs requiring the clubs of policemen and the bayoneted M-1 rifles of National Guardsmen. I had seen violence permeate the fabric of our society from small town lynchings to urban race wars, endemic assassinations that cut down political leaders of all persuasions and rule of law in a state of turmoil.

By 1978 criminal justice was not swift. The moral conscience of our society was in a debate with itself – the inequities of swift justice weighed against the burdensome and lengthy rights of appeal and the emerging issues of civil rights. In 1976 the reinstatement of the death penalty in Texas revived that moral dilemma. Rape was no longer a capital offense. Racially biased rhetoric was unprintable.

I sought out Clarendon citizens who remembered the rape case. There were few. Not so few in the number of those who had lived there then but few in the number of those who remembered it. Of the three court appointed attorneys for the defense of Morris Norman, J. Ralph Porter, W. J. Link and John Knorpp, only Knorpp survived in 1979. In our correspondence with him he only vaguely remembered the details of the case but clearly remembered that "this case set the 'world's record' for swift justice. He got the death penalty and was sent to the electric chair." A cryptic note from the County Clerk stated that courthouse records of the case would be difficult if not impossible to locate. [8]

Research in the seventies was time consuming. It meant traveling to libraries in Amarillo and Canyon where hours were spent fingering through card index files and pulling actual books and journal articles off of the shelves. Rewards for those efforts had proved to be meager. There seemed to be little to no information about the questions I had about the death penalty and its execution. Had it served as a deterrent? Had society been made safer by the death of those who offended against it? Did dragging it out endlessly serve justice or prolong the suffering of the families of the victims and of the perpetrators? The bulk of that which came off of the library shelves was the bitter debate involving the fair and humane treatment of the offenders.

At that time my personal experience had involved the suffering of victims as the new appeal systems prolonged the final execution of a death penalty. I had stood by my cousins as they lived out their lives suspended between hope for a final decision and dread of a prolonged retrial of the same offense. I also felt a sense compassion for the cruelty of sentencing a man to live out his natural life waiting on death row.

A first response to the shattering of innocence is disillusionment. As a child I had seen how docile house dogs became vicious marauders when they joined the pack. As an adult I had seen the mob spirit unleashed in human beings. The embers of the 60's may have cooled but the smoke of dissent and racial bitterness still hung heavy in the air of the 70's. By 1978 space travel was no longer fantasy. Space wars between Russia and the western world were a looming possibility. An invasion by Martians would not have seemed impossible. If the historic significance of Orson Welles' broadcast had been that it predicted all of this, again he had taken it from H. G. Wells who wrote in 1895 from his travels aboard *The Time Machine*:

"What if cruelty had grown into a common passion? What if in this interval the race had lost its manliness, and had developed into something inhuman, unsympathetic, and overwhelmingly powerful?" [9]

There was no doubt. Mankind was engulfed in cruelty and there seemed to be no solution for it. For the time being in 1978 I missed the significance of something else prophetic - the sound of an actor's voice reaching out to millions through electronic sound waves that sent two weeping and hysterical women in Providence, Rhode Island to seek consolation from a newspaper telephone line[10] while in Clarendon at that same hour there were two weeping and hysterical women covered in their own blood seeking help from a neighbor.[11] The community rallied around them, brought the matter to a swift conclusion and closed the file. Though still uncertain about the meaning of my father's prayer, in 1978, I, too, closed the file drawer on my newspaper clippings and left the story suspended in time.

I was more intrigued with the writings of H.G. Wells that had inspired the historic radio broadcast, *War of the Worlds and Other Stories*, specifically *The Time Machine*. It was Wells' genius to synthesize reality and scientific fact with imagination and make plausible the most outlandish ideas. Over time scientific possibilities naturally become reality often enough to add to his credibility as a prophet. The depth of his understanding of the nature of man added the universal quality that made him classic.

With the creation of the idea of the time machine he could tap into the yearning of all mankind to take control of time and move about in it with the same facility as moving about the depth, breadth and height of space. Time was the Fourth Dimension of space that made a cube of it:

"It must have length, breadth, thickness, and – duration. . . .Can a cube that does not last for any time at all, have a real existence? "

Convincingly, he reminded how our consciousness moves along time from the beginning to the end of our lives. So why, then, cannot we move in time as we move about in the other dimensions of Space, accelerate the drift along the Time-Dimension, or even turnabout and travel the other way? It would be remarkably convenient for the historian, he argued, to travel back and verify, amplify. As for the future, another speculated, the investor could leave all of his money to accumulate interest and speed on ahead to spend it. And so Wells spun his tale about the Time Machine that with a touch to the lever would create a rush of wind, extinguish the lights and disappear into a whirling mass of dust, broken glass and bits of black and brass and speed forward or backward into time at will. In truth, the universality of Wells' argument is man's enduring wish to counter his mortality with fantasies of conquering the fleeting quality of time. Wells' theory was not a valid scientific one. Einstein's theory of relativity was published soon thereafter and his fanciful notion of the fourth dimension of time was dismissed. What did endure was the poignant love story of the Time Traveler and Little Weena.

She was one of the surviving species of mankind he called the Eloi. He had seen her swept away in a river current and drowning in full view of her fellowman. In their apathy and self-complacency they did nothing to save her. The Time Traveler saved her and for the rest of his sojourn to the year 802,701 AD she danced at his side stuffing exotic white flowers into his pockets and showering him with kisses of gratitude and tenderness.[12] The sad ending to their story leaves the reader wishing to return in time and save their love. Of course that was no more possible than for me to have returned to type my name into a newspaper article.

▲ ▲ ▲

By the eve of Halloween, 2011, when I returned to the story, I was into the third decade of a career as a professional counselor where I was in daily contact with man's cruelty and its victims. Sustaining me through those years were the enduring memories of my blissful childhood, my Buttercup years. Near the desk in my bedroom was the chair that had always been nearby, the old cane bottom chair. It had travelled with me along the Fourth-Dimension of my entire life. It was the chair my mother sat on during the remarkable events of my childhood. It was the stadium seat in our yard for my aerobatic performances with the swing. It was the nurse's chair at my bedside when I was sick. On summer nights it was small enough for mother to sit under the bare bulb light over the thirty inch square piece of concrete, the front door step that was also our front porch.   We formed a circle around mother and the chair. Daddy squatted on the lawn in the way that men did in those days – suspended in the air on the way down to the ground as though sitting upon an invisible stool six inches high. I kneeled in the grass beside him and my brother, Lloyd, romped about us.

On those evenings my parents entertained themselves by seeing my brother and I watch a very large frog, so fat he could not hop, waddle up to the porch and run out his long tongue to snare the insects that swarmed under the light. We squealed with delight each time, like a rubber band, he popped his tongue and a bug back into his mouth.

The old cane bottomed chair. Funny, now it was not even that. The cane bottom had given out long ago. There had been a variety of bottoms and many different coats of paint as it blended into the décor of whatever day. I caressed the skinned corner of the back where the layers of paint were chronicled like growth rings in a tree stump. At the very beginning it was a dark wood stain. Green was the color of that fateful night. It had been aluminum grey when Neil Armstrong set foot on the moon. Tonight it was blue. In whatever era the old chair brought me enduring memories of my mother and it anchored me each time I braved the entrance into a new epoch of my life.

On my desk was my computer, a glittering metallic rectangle scarcely larger than a notepad. On the screen were images sent from Mars by the spaceship *Curiosity,* the latest in the now common explorations of that planet. The fantasies of yesteryears were the realities of the present. Suddenly I realized that in my hand I held an actual time machine. Still intimidated by such advanced technology, I typed in the name of Morris Norman and to my amazement four results filled my screen. At the top of the screen the date was October 30, 2011. Three quarters of a century later something about that human being had endured. I opened the search and found an excerpt from a recently published book about death row in the Texas Prison System. Taken from a letter written by a neighbor and longtime acquaintance of Norman it read:

"I will say that this is a sad surprise to me and others who knew Morris Norman #208 (that he) is charged with rape; this negro boy has worked for me at different times around my home with my wife and daughter at home and I being away from home lots of times all day. We know nothing against him and have at all times found him a well behaved humble negro boy. . . ." [13]

As though no distance had intervened upon the image etched into my memory, I saw my father's head bowed in prayer over a newspaper spread before him on the green kitchen table. On November 3, 1938 *The Donley County Leader* read:

"Morris Norman, 20 year old smug, pretentious, Illinois Negro in jail cell in Amarillo, is today awaiting the outcome of an indictment charging him with criminal assault of a Clarendon white woman here last Sunday night ... Termed the most brutal attack in the history of the southland, Norman, with no remorse on his ebony hued face, signed a lurid written confession. [14]

In the space of less than two years the well behaved humble Negro boy had transformed into a cold blooded rapist.[15] How could that have been? In the space of a few seconds I was now the historian obsessed with traveling back to verify, amplify. I was a clinician in search of etiologies. The lever to my time machine was now simply a mouse to my computer.

3

The Setting

In 1938 THE atmospheric conditions in the society and in the political and legal systems of Texas were just the accumulation of
opposing forces needed to send up a tall, black dust devil when they
collided over a dump ground in Clarendon, Texas. A dust devil
danced about furiously for forty-six days, sucked in an array of human lives and their opposing ideologies and slammed them together
vigorously. Then the dust devil dissipated as quickly as it formed.
Debris from the particles involved was strewn about willy-nilly in ob-
scure hiding places and went virtually unnoticed for decades. Re-
examination of the particles calls for an understanding of the fuel
that ignited the spin.

The decade following World War I, The Roaring Twenties, saw
more change in the economic and social makeup of Clarendon and
Donley County than in any other era in its previous history. The radio, telephone and automobile became commonplace. World news
was broadcast as it happened. Barriers of distance were removed from
human interchange. Suddenly, Donley County was becoming a part
of the greater world. Down state the old style plantation production

of cotton was breaking up and small farm cotton production moved into the Panhandle edging into the vast grasslands of the big ranches that had originally brought civilization to the area. Creating a need for black field workers small black communities sprang up in formally all white communities and this class of blacks was added to the small but already established colored town of Clarendon. [1] Old South values standards were being tested by the changes in economic structures and by a national discontent with a wave of postwar crime and decline in traditional morality. The resulting tension provided ideal conditions to attract the new Ku Klux Klan. The new Klan was not the Klan of the Reconstruction days but a movement standing for community altruism, law and order and the moral values of Victorian America. [2]

In 1922 the Klan made its appearance in Clarendon with a rush of appearances fostering Victorian standards of morality and charitable benevolences. During 1922 a steady flow of articles were seen in *The Clarendon News*, "KKK Donates to the Red Cross." December 15, 1921, "KKK Visits Baptist Church," March 2, 1922,"Donation by KKK to Poor Widow in Giles," March 16, 1922, "KKK Appears at Gholdstone Church Revival," August 3, 1922, "KKK Makes Donation at Goodnight Methodist Church," August 24, 1922.

In June 1922, the whole community greeted a spectacular parade with mounted Klansmen carrying their fiery cross behind Old Glory. "Thousands Witness Parade of the Ku Klux Klan in Clarendon. . ." One hundred and seventy robed and hooded Klansmen marched two abreast behind the mounted flagman bearing Old Glory followed by the fiery cross. Mayor Cagle officially viewed the parade from a parade stand erected for the occasion. The crowd, said to have numbered five thousand, applauded as the horseman passed by marching down Kearney Street to the White's house before turning east and dispersing as mysteriously as it had appeared." [3]

The people of Clarendon loved parades. The people of Clarendon still love parades. Parades are a Clarendon legacy. But this Klan parade had a peculiar intrigue. It was vibrant with patriotism and honor for Old Glory still fresh from The Great War. It was sanctified with pulpit thumping rhetoric extolling moral purity. And the Klansmen were slight of hand magicians. The fiery cross appeared menacing and the Klansmen waved it to hear gasps from the crowd. It had actually been soaked in kerosene, the fuel for the common kerosene lantern that produced a flame burning light but did not burn the lantern wick. In order to carry off the impression that the Klansmen just mysteriously vanished, they waved the cross vigorously to distract the crowd's attention to how they took off their robes one by one, tucked them out of sight and mingled into the crowd.

In August of that year a half page ad in the *Clarendon News* addressed "To The Lovers of Law and Order" declared that Knights of the Ku Klux Klan, No., 165 of the Realm of Texas was officially in Clarendon, Texas with an active membership of 200. It set forth a zealous pledge to uphold the constitution of the United Sates, protect its flag, to support a free school system, maintain white supremacy, protect pure womanhood and abolish mob violence. Bootleggers, gamblers, woman-chasers, hi-jackers and hot-check artists were warned to get an honest job and become good citizens. [4]

These moral values resonated soundly with the religious standards upon which the original town of Clarendon was established as a "Christian community" in 1878 by the Methodist minister Reverend Lewis Henry Carhart. The early town leaders so carefully managed the few saloons and so prohibited any of the rowdy behavior of cowboys who wandered through that the boisterous, thrill-seeking class of cowboys gave the town its nickname of Saint's Roost and steered clear of it.

*Matthew R "Bones" Hooks (1867-1951) Clarendon
pioneer, Amarillo civic leader and founder of the "white
flower tribute." photo by Ernest L. Hunt, 1943.*

Ironically, it was this reputation that brought the first blacks to New
Clarendon through the person of Matthew, "Bones" Hooks. He liked
the God-fearing town. "Clarendon," he said, "was the white spot of civilization. Prohibition started there, colleges started there, everything
good got its start in Clarendon. He maintained this view of Clarendon

even though as a black man he was initially not allowed to stay there. It took several years and several persistent attempts, but he was eventually accepted by the residents and allowed to buy a small plot of land and build a home. In the same quiet way of earning the respect and friendship of the ranchers for whom he broke and trained horses, in 1894 the town fathers agreed to let Bones have land for a Negro church. He brought in a preacher from Ft. Worth and from the few blacks in the area who worked in the homes of wealthier whites, he assembled both a beginning congregation and a small black community. As the first black church and the first such community established in the Panhandle the colored section of Clarendon had its own Saint's Roost image. [5]

Bones Hooks' high moral image extended beyond Clarendon and beyond his lifetime. Today he is still remembered for his "lone white flower" tribute, a symbolic tribute of honor bestowed, in his words, ". . . to whom honor is due." Over the years, recipients of the flower were Panhandle pioneers, local citizens and even national dignitaries.[6] Individually, he awarded them to Franklin and Eleanor Roosevelt.[7]

Under the hood Donley county Klansmen could brandish the fiery cross and chant moral virtues and white supremacy but in their daily lives they were farmers and merchants who depended upon the services of the black people. The black community survived.

As the zealous agenda of the new Klan played out, law enforcement and the criminal justice system suffered the most. There were instances where the Klan's pledge to intervene upon arrests of blacks and to punish lawyers with black clients were actually carried out.[8]

This would directly affect R. Y. King shortly after he returned from his service in World War I to resume his law practice in Hedley. He had been court appointed to represent a black criminal in trial. The duty of any member of the bar is to fulfill this right to counsel as he would for any client even though he receives no fee. In this spirit King took the case. Almost immediately he began receiving letters from the Klan warning him that he would be hanged if he continued to represent the black man.

Still single at that time, King lived in the Hedley Hotel on the second floor. Determined to honor his civic and statutory duty, he devised a plan to insure his safety. During the day he was armed with a revolver. At night he rigged an alarm to warn him if anyone tried to enter his room. Filling the lid to a syrup can with small rocks, he propped it into the transom window over the door to his room in such a way that it would fall and send the rocks spilling noisily onto the floor if anyone opened the door. He slept with the revolver under his pillow. The outcome was that King's client was found guilty and duly sentenced. King's next word from the Klan was in the form of a postcard featuring the picture of fully robed Klansmen with the handwritten invitation to join their membership.[9]

KU KLUX
(In Full Uniform)

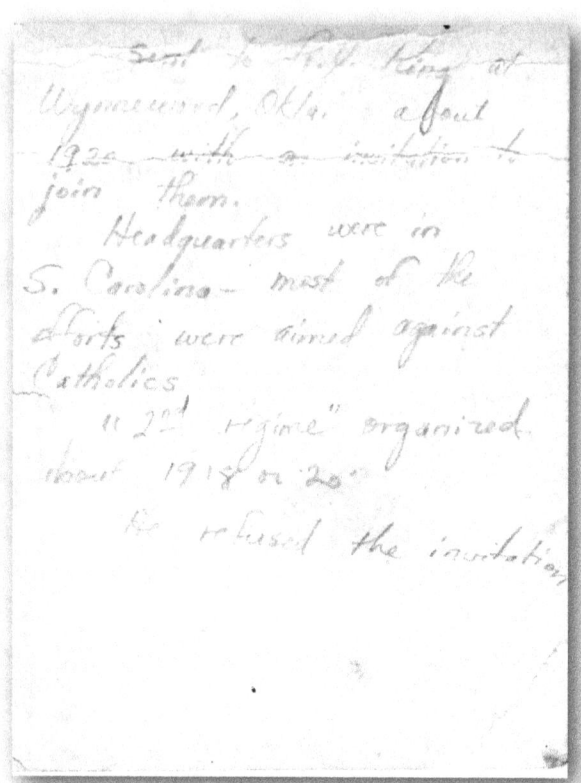

Ku Klux Klan Postcard received by R. Y. King after he returned to his law practice from service in World War I sometime after 1920. Historic notations made on the back of the card by family members.

When Ku Klux rallies began to occur sporadically in Memphis as they did in Clarendon in the 1920's, attorney and future District Attorney, John Deaver, utilized his humor to minimize the power of the Klan. When he had an audience of several citizens he would remind them that people in Hall County were too poor to own more than one pair of shoes, so that it was not hard to tell who was under the hood and robe. Obviously surveying the shoes of those among his audience and matching each pair to a face with a motion of his head, he left them with his typical good natured laugh.[10]

Showy sightings of robed Klansmen and fiery crosses in the Panhandle died down as the Klan took on quite a different image in other parts of the state. There the Klan launched a reign of terror upon offenders of the Klan's moral codes. Hooded gangs whipped or tarred and feathered adulterers, bootleggers and attorneys with black or criminal clients. In the sites of many of these atrocities peace officers looked the other way or even under the hood took part in the savagery.[11] This image of the Klan began to overshadow the noble charitable and moral image. Not wishing to be identified with such violence, the Klansmen's shoes in the Panhandle dispersed out into the communities without the hoods and public fanfare. Presence of the Klan was only in the form of rumor or anonymous letters. As an underground movement to enforce its stern codes it became more ominous. In one of the rural communities where the robed activities had previously been prominent it was rumored that a secret lynching had occurred. The sheriff's department investigated the rumor but never found enough evidence to make a case on it.[12]

In May of 1930 Guy Pierce won the democratic nomination for the office of Donley County Sheriff. By then Texans' romantic notions about their Old Western style of keeping law and order were changing. The image of the local sheriff as the "lone ranger" with his six-shooter and sure fire "silver bullet" or the "one riot, one Ranger" image of state law enforcement were no longer adequate. For a decade or more leaders in the larger law enforcement community had been calling for reform. As one Ranger put it, "Why, we're still in the horseback stage while crime travels in 85-a-mile cars," Crime was on the rise. On the average there was at least one bank robbery in the State of Texas every day. Bandits were well equipped with high-powered weapons and bullet-proof cars.[13] The average rural county sheriff was no match for the modern criminal. Struggling with the Great Depression, neither was the average county budget.

Clarendon took pride in its high per capita ratio of church buildings to the population and its low crime rate. Naively cloaked in its Saint's Roost image the citizenry of Clarendon could believe that adherence to its Ten Commandment values would shield it from the bank robberies, cattle rustling rings, speakeasies, lynch mobs and the political corruption in Austin that plagued other parts of the state. Overlooked in the same way, despite the proclamations of the Klan and stern sermons from the community's pulpits, was the clandestine bootlegging and other sporting activities that existed in its midst. Local law enforcement officers were expected to contain these, too, in traditional "horse and buggy" style. In Clarendon the principle of containment meant keep crime in control but keep it out sight and north of the railroad tracks, or at least reputed to be kept there. "The oldest profession" existed on both sides of the tracks. Rumors had it that the white girls were transient residents of the Antro Hotel who were made "to move on" when discovered[14] while the black girls were hometown girls who operated out of their homes.[15]

Bootlegging also existed on both sides of the track. It was excused by creating a kind of folkloric image for it. A white bootlegger who operated on the streets of Clarendon from his wheelchair was the jovial sort and he was tolerated with a kind of benevolence. There was a more flamboyant image in colored town for Marble Eye, "the Kingfish" of the black bootleggers. Clarendon could maintain its Saint's Roost image and wink at the rest. It took a horrific tragedy in downstate Sherman, Texas, to rattle this complacency.

On May 9 in Sherman a black field hand angry about six dollars owed him by his employer had repeatedly raped his employer's wife while her five year old son had looked on in horror. He had been quickly apprehended, had readily confessed and was scheduled for a speedy trial in a second-floor courtroom in the courthouse guarded by several deputies and five Texas Rangers. Failing to heed the grim reminders of the "Waco Horror" courthouse lynching in 1916, the Rangers underestimated the hoard of angry whites that stormed the hallways of the courthouse and pushed against the courtroom door while the trial was in progress. An unscrupulous newsman was in the crowd circulating a bogus telegram from Governor Dan Moody ordering lead Texas Ranger, Frank Hamer, not to shoot into the crowd. Uncertain of the veracity of the telegram and not wanting to cause injury to the whites, Hamer reportedly had refrained from firing into them. He fired shots in the air and in the last tragic moments peppered some with buckshot but he failed to deter the mob. The tragic ending to this incident was that the white mobsters, 5000 in number, burned their own courthouse to the ground along with many homes and businesses in the black community. The Rangers were unable to save the prisoner or to prevent the mob from stealing his body, dragging it through the streets of the black community before hanging and torching it as it hung by the feet from a Cottonwood tree.

Three weeks later in the neighboring town of Honey Grove another lynching ended the life of another young black who had killed his overseer over a wage dispute. The people of Honey Grove were relying upon their own sheriff to take care of the matter and the assemblage of citizenry that became the mob was a self-appointed posse there to help him. The black youth who had barricaded himself was killed during the standoff with lawmen. Imitating the mob savagery seen in the Sherman affair, the mob robbed the dead body of the black youth, dragged it through the streets, mutilated it and finally hanged it and doused it with gasoline and burned it. The 1930 cases had horrified law abiding citizens of Texas. They had served as both embarrassment and inspiration to the law enforcement community.

A spirit of rugged individualism and self-sufficiency had also existed in the neighboring counties of Wheeler and Collingsworth when on July 11, 1930 the wife of a prominent Wheeler County farmer was bludgeoned to death in her home by a 21 year old black farm hand in what was alleged to have been an attempted rape. The sheriff in nearby Wellington quickly responded to the call and quickly arrested the murderer and within hours had obtained his confession. He and the sheriff of Wheeler County, where the crime actually occurred, communicated by telephone to conceal the whereabouts of the murderer. But they had failed at the onset to portray a unified and commanding image to the public so that those who felt obligated to avenge the crime more immediately gained the advantage. What followed was five days in which area peace officers had to skirt the young black from jail to jail through back roads in the night throughout the eastern Panhandle and western Oklahoma to elude clusters of white lynch mobs that gathered intent on stealing and lynching him before he could be safely jailed, arraigned and prepared for a trial.

It was not until five days after the crime that the local lawmen realized that they could not manage this situation alone. They called in the Texas Rangers. Legendary "Lone Wolf" Gonzaullas and three other Rangers were sent from Austin to take charge of the Wellington/Shamrock case. While the flashy and vain style of riot management Gonzuallas enacted in this case was designed to correct the mistakes made in the tragedies of the Sherman and Honey Grove riots, it proved to be inappropriate in the Shamrock/Wellington case.

During the controversy following the Sherman riot, Gonzaullas had gained national headlines when he quipped that the Ranger in charge should simply have "shot the hell out of the mob and then at once called for more help." The Shamrock case provided him the opportunity to make a grandiose show of strength aimed at disarming the mob spirit. He sped ahead of the car carrying the Wellington suspect to the Pampa jail and "unloaded a conspicuous display of armament – machine guns, rifles, shotguns, pistols, and grenades." Word went out into all of the communities involved that the prisoner's safety would be secured "regardless of the cost." The murderer was brought to trial and with the same arsenal in sight in the court room, Ranger Gonzuallas shielded him from the sight of courtroom spectators with his person. On July 28, 1930, Jesse Lee Washington, ironically, a relative of the Jesse Washington lynched in the 1916 "Waco Horror," was convicted of murder and given the death sentence. On September 12, two months and one day after the crime, he was executed.

But in Shamrock the whole affair had left the white community embittered by the way the case was handled by the Rangers. There, as in Clarendon, public sentiment was still aligned with the "peculiar chivalry" of the South. It was a Christian mandate that women, white women, be protected. An overriding code of honor among southern men was that any insult to the virtue of womanhood be avenged by death to the perpetrator. Justified by these beliefs, an impassioned telegram was sent to Governor Moody by fifteen white ladies from Shamrock. Claiming to speak for all white women in Texas they condemned the governor for threatening to kill the men that were acting to uphold their honor and safety in order to protect "a confessed Negro rapist and murderer." [16]

Four years into Guy Pierce's tenure of office James V. Allred was elected Governor of Texas running on a platform for the creation of a modern state police force. Pierce would play a role as this force evolved and became a reality in the Panhandle area. Throughout the legislative process of creating the new Department of Public Safety, the Sheriff's Association of Texas had played a leading role in promoting the interests of the local sheriff in Texas and advocating for his inclusion as a participant in the new comprehensive system of law enforcement.

In keeping with Allred's dream of a state of the art state police force the plan enacted by the 1936 Legislation was a sound plan. But for the first few years implementation of the plan was snagged up in execution of the fifth part of the plan – removal of Peace Officers from influence or control by politicians. The ensuing jockeying for power among the leadership of the Department had kept Homer Garrison contained in the position of Assistant Director until September 24, 1938 when Director Horace Carmichael suddenly died of a heart attack. On September 28, 1938 Garrison was officially named as DPS Director.[17] On September 29, 1938 the *Amarillo Globe* ran a story detailing Garrison's move to redesign and strengthen the DPS in the Panhandle area.

R. M. Hammett, veteran peace officer, was promoted to the rank of sergeant and assigned to work under Captain Jim Line who headed up the Panhandle district of the DPS. Andrew Baker, another veteran patrolman, was also assigned to the district. These men would join Ranger Neal Arthur who had served in Amarillo as Senior Criminal Investigator with the Bureau of Intelligence since 1937. Arthur, Line and Baker all joined the Highway Patrol on the same day in 1932 at its inception as a law enforcement branch. Hammett joined the patrol only a few months later. Over the years all four of these men had worked together in law enforcement and criminal investigation.[18]

Another Ranger assigned as Junior Criminal Investigator to the Amarillo area earlier in the year was Pat Taliaferro. Interestingly, when the DPS was formed in 1935, the notorious "Lone Wolf" Gonzuellas had left the limelight as a Ranger in the enforcement service to head up the Bureau of Intelligence. In this behind the scenes role he brought the Department into line with all of the latest in the scientific methods of criminal investigation. These new methods would also include updated methods of interrogation and more beneficial communication with the public. His primary role was to train investigators in the Department such as Rangers Arthur and Taliaferro.[19]

In his persona Ranger Arthur carried the image of the quiet, polite patrolman and behind the scenes investigator. One acquaintance described him as "quiet as a clam."[20] Taliaferro carried quite a different image. In his youth in Seymour he was known as a dashing young man with adventuresome ways of driving a car.[21] During his early career as a deputy in Seymour and Abilene he often garnered the headlines with stories of his notorious criminal arrests and investigations.[22] As a Ranger in 1939 he took part in a daring shoot out with a fugitive from justice.[23] Ranger Taliaferro's driving skills were a match for the 85-mile-an hour armor plated criminal. By mid-October, 1938, Director Garrison had given the Amarillo area company status, Texas Rangers, Company "E", Amarillo. Rangers Arthur and Taliaferro were its criminal investigators. This brought the total number of state police in the Panhandle district to 23, the team put in place to serve the Amarillo area just two weeks before the Clarendon rape case would occur. [24]

By October, 1938, it was the state police force that the Donley County Sheriff had to work with. It was a team he was a member of. His experience and involvement in law enforcement in the whole eastern Panhandle was an asset to the team and to his district. Guy Pierce would lead the team in a show of law enforcement efficiency that would serve as a test case for Homer Garrison's vision.

On Halloween Eve, 1938, children guised as world dignitaries left the dress rehearsal of the Tom Thumb Wedding and returned home with their parents. Orson Welles' radio voice, unnoticed in Clarendon, terrified the rest of the nation. At 9:30 p.m., Sheriff Guy Pierce answered the telephone call that initiated the real life tale of horror.

4

Appointment in Clarendon

U NAWARE THAT THEY were already particles being gathered into the swirl appointed to meet in Clarendon in 1938, two school teachers went about their daily lives during the fall of 1930.

Stylishly attired in a pastel floral frock, silk hose and fashion hat, Cora Ferris stepped aboard the school transport boat, the *W.E.D.*, as it began its daily trip down the upper bayou picking up the children and dropping them off at the Comardelle Village School where she taught. Cora was a boarder in the home of W.E., "Duffy," and Agnes Dufrene of Des Allemands, St. Charles Parish, Louisiana. "Duffy" was owner and captain of the school boat, *W.E.D.*, and as jury police or "ward boss", he was responsible for the ward school system. As this water world's only link to the civilization of the dry land world, he also delivered the mail, small house goods and the all-important French bread. Just 30 miles from New Orleans and the great Mississippi River, the ward was a world of lakes, swamps and a major bayou that connected Lake Des Allemands to Lake Salvador. People lived on high spots along the bayou or in house boats tied to the wharves. Comardelle Village was midway down the bayou centrally located in a prime fishing and trapping area. During the peak of the trapping season, houseboats of as many as 30 families were tied to the wharves all along the bayou. Before 1925 when the pink school house was barged there from Des Allemandes, some 100 children paddled a pirogue or skiff to the village and with it docked at the wharf, attended school in private homes. Few of the children spoke English. Most of the fishermen and trappers were of Arcadian French origin. Moss gatherers and woodsmen who cut the Cyprus for lumber or to burn into charcoal to be sold in New Orleans were German. Eventually the cultures blended and became known as the Cajuns who spoke English with their unique accent. They broadened the sources of their off season income to include frogging, hunting alligators or market duck hunting.

With all of his accomplishments for the education system of the area, "Duffy's" most memorable legacy was the boardwalk he personally build to connect the wharves to the school so that the student's feet could stay dry on their way to the four room pink schoolhouse during high tide or low. It is said that he placed this as a priority over using the money to build roads. In those days there were very few roads in the entire parish.

Cora joined the school in 1925 when it and the *W. E. D.* were created. With all of the children off of the boats at the Cormadelle wharf and up the boardwalks, Cora began her school day in the four room school where she taught the upper grades, officially in English, but actually in whatever dialect her students understood.[1]

The vast water world of Comardelle Village was an interesting contrast to the expansive grassy prairies of southwestern Oklahoma near Altus. Here in the shadows of the seven steep peaks of the Navajo Mountains rising abruptly out of an endless stretch of arid grassland, Cora was born and finished High School. [2]

Schoolteachers, Cora Ferris and Marguerite Brandt, board the W.E.R.
for their daily trip down the bayou to their school at Comardelle Village.

In the Texas Panhandle on the flats near the JA Ranch Headquarters Maggie Scoggins pulled a pair of bib overalls over her "school marm" dress and mounted the horse saddled for her each morning by the son of her landlords, the Wylies. With her lunch sack stuffed under the bib she rode three miles alongside the JA bull pasture to the one room Palo Duro School located on Griffin Flats. This school served the families that farmed the ranch feed crops located on the flats and did the ranch work that was centered at Headquarters. Here the ranch maintained the brood mares and their colts, broke the broncs and managed the registered bulls. In the fall the shipper calves were assembled at Headquarters and trailed to Ashtola where they would be sent to market by train.

Her students, six to eight in number, were all ages, no more than two in the same grade. With their horses hobbled or hitched to a cedar post, they assembled around the pot bellied wood stove to "thaw out" from their own ride until they heard the hand held bell that called them to their desks. Built for two, the slanted desktops hinged over a bin for books, pencils, pens, ink bottles, rulers, compasses and art gum erasers. During her school day Maggie went from desk to desk giving and hearing assignments from the individual grade level textbooks. Her recess duties included watching for rattlesnakes that occasionally visited the playground and reminding her students to pick up all particles of food left from their lunch sacks so as to avoid inviting coyotes to visit the playground looking for the leftovers.

Maggie Belle Scoggins, "school marm" at Palo Duro School, 1929, attired for her morning ride in coveralls over a floral frock. Photo by Ernest L. Hunt.

Maggie grew up hearing "wild bull stories" from her father, Jim Scoggins, Armstrong County Road Commissioner. He dynamited the original Koogle Falloff road into Headquarters flats through the JJ bull pasture. He could tell exciting stories about his encounters with those bulls and Maggie never learned to trust a barbed wire fence that separated her from the bulls who sometimes decided to travel along side of her on her morning ride to school. On those days the students could have had the school to themselves if Bill Wyle had not escorted her horseback through the danger zone.

At her Christmas break Maggie married Ernest Hunt whom she had originally met when he boarded in her home as a member of the construction crew that built the Mount Pleasant School near her home. Being 14 years her senior, Ernest had waited for her to "grow up" before asking her to be his bride. Sitting on the doorstep of the school house, she accepted his marriage proposal on the condition that she could finish her school year.

Consistent with the customs of that time, they stood alone before a Baptist minister, said their vows and went home. As a part of the local customs they would be surprised there by their friends with a shivery, a party to celebrate the wedding. Large banners draped over the front porch of the small red brick house teased the honeymooners. One that read, "The longest night of the year," surrounded with pictures of hearts pierced with arrows referred to their wedding date, December 22, the equinox. After refreshments they were showered with gifts of household items and furniture. Among these gifts was the cane-bottomed chair.

A typical date for Ernest Hunt and Maggie Belle Scoggins during Maggie's senior year in Claude High School, a Sunday afternoon outing in his Ford sedan.

When Ernest Hunt returned from World War I to his parent's home in Clarendon, he pursued a career in carpentry. But when there was a slump in the housing market preceding the Stock Market crash of 1929, he sought other work. Ernest was hired by the US Postal Service.

During the spring of 1930, Maggie boarded in the home of Mae and "Boy" Blackwell during the week, Ernest worked in the Post Office and the couple spent their weekends in their little red brick home in Clarendon.

Another May-December romance, that of Deputy Sheriff Guy Pierce and Mary Peabody, added more newlyweds to the young couples of Clarendon. Their romance had a western flair. They met when she became, at age 17, the youngest jailer in the State of Texas and he was a deputy sheriff for Donley County.[3] It was an eventful year for Pierce. In May he won the Democratic nomination for Donley County Sheriff. In June he was drawn with other area lawmen into the Wellington/Shamrock affair. That same year the Sheriff's department was involved in a crisis typical of the Depression Era.

There was threat of a run on the county bank. Rumors that the bank was failing had caused an ugly and nervous crowd to line up in the street in front of the bank. The men were ready to demand their money, each trying to get his before the money was gone. Some cowhands in the line wore side arms. In a test of mob control the sheriff, his deputies and the county judge, J. Ralph Porter, stood before the bank doors.

Porter was a small, quiet man with poor eyesight. The strong correction in his glasses made his eyes appear to stand out from his face giving everyone in a large group of people the feeling that his eyes were looking directly into their face. He may have actually not been able to see every face at all but he had a unique way of connecting with others. The genius of his leadership was in his ability to motivate and empower others to carry out his mission thinking it was their own.

The judge climbed up on a wagon and held up his hands and the crowd quieted. He assured them that the bank had more than enough money to give each his share. He suggested that they calm down and go home. This argument failed to calm their panic. He tried another line of reasoning and began suggesting that having their money out of the bank made them target for robberies.

"While you are sleeping someone could knock you in the head and steal your money."

Now, Porter had their attention. He offered a solution. He suggested they invest the money they took from the bank into Government savings bonds instead. Generously, he offered personal or deputy escort to the Post Office. One by one he personally escorted each man who followed his suggestion to the Post Office making himself and his mission as conspicuous as possible. Others followed his example until a steady line of men, each with his life savings in hand and a deputy standing nearby, were waiting in line at the Post Office clerks' windows.

By means of a prearranged plan between the Post Office and the bank, the money was finding its way out of the back door of the Post Office into the back door of the bank and into the Postmaster's Post Office account. The bank patrons' money was safely invested, the U. S. Treasury got a boost and the local bank survived. [4]

That evening, bridegroom Pierce bragged to his jailer bride about how his escort service had saved her the job of having to book her jail full of rioters. Postal clerk Hunt quietly teased his bride about how he had run more money through his cash tray that day than the both of them would see again in a lifetime. The county judge retired that night knowing that he had saved the people of his county a total loss of their savings and a gruesome series of foreclosures and evictions. But nothing would spare the citizens of Donley County the grim future they faced as the Great Depression deepened.

After the November general election, Guy and Mary Pierce moved into the jail. Mary was no longer a hired jailer. As wife of the sheriff she was now automatically an in house jailer. The prisoners were locked in their cells on the second story. She and her family lived in the first floor. Mary cooked for the prisoners and when needed, functioned as their guard.[5] Sheriff Pierce and County Judge Porter had to work together to check the hungry and homeless from finding easy access to Mary's source of food and shelter. When the sheriff had to arrest some of these, the judge would levy a fine of having to do manual work for the county in lieu of jail time.[6]

Postal workers took a 50% cut in pay. For Ernest Hunt this meant that his $150.00 per month pay check was cut to $75.00. Even so, he was among the lucky. He had a job with a steady income. In order to make this cover the needs of his young family, however, he purchased a 20 acre farm at the eastern edge of Clarendon where he and Maggie could raise chickens for meat and eggs and keep a milk cow for milk, butter and the barter income from cream.

The school at Comardelle was discontinued sometime after 1941. The four room school house was barged up the bayou to Des Allemands and eventually became the American Legion hall there. The *W.E.D.* brought the students up the Bayou to a new school.[7] Cora resigned her position to join her sister, Mattie, in Clarendon after the death of Mr. Jones. She slipped into Clarendon virtually unnoticed. Nothing was known about her career as school teacher. She was Mrs. Jones' younger sister who came to help her with the truck farm. She was known only to a few for her affiliation with the church where they spoke in tongues.

5

At the Vortex

As THE SINISTER tones of Orson Welles' voice were terrifying millions sitting before their radio sets over the nation, the crisp autumn air settling over Clarendon was filled with the melodic outpouring of human voices. These were not sounds of fear but of religious ecstasy drifting out of the windows of a rectangular box shaped church building in the eastern part of town. This congregation, relatively new to the community, was known for its charismatic services where the members continued "singing in the spirit" long after all of the other congregations in town had ended their Sunday evening worship services and gone home. They "rejoiced, shouted, talked in tongues, danced, and prophesied." Their services were melodic. The sermons, Scripture readings, songs and prayers were chanted in chorus. At the conclusion they left amid exchanges of handshakes and embraces and drifted in family groups out into the night.[1]

Cora Ferris was known for her affiliation with the Assembly of God Church and her fervor for the movement it represented. Soon after her arrival in Clarendon she became a part of a small group of worshippers who first met in a room in the Denver Hotel just north of the railroad station and later became the charter members of The First Assembly of God of Clarendon.[2]

Notable to the history of the establishment of the Assembly of God Church in the South were events in Biloxi 1922 at the same time she began the school year as Assistant Principle to the Harrison-Jackson County Line School on the back bay of Biloxi. A September revival that was highlighted by the river baptism of 75 converts and the founding of the Central Assembly of God Church of Biloxi at the corner of Division and Lee streets was just three-quarters of a mile from her home at 501 Maple. Every morning she walked past the beginning construction of the first permanent home of that church to catch the ferry and ride a mile across the Bay to the D'Iberville ferry landing and her little green school. There she taught the young "hosses from across," a term used in Biloxi to describe that French speaking community on the back bay. 1922 was also the year that a mystic, who wore a long white beard and calling himself Brother Isaiah and his followers lived in houseboats and tents in the St. Martin area served by this school. Brother Isaiah gained national notoriety for his preaching and miraculous healing.[3]

In Cormadelle Village, Cora's proximity to a newly established Assembly of God Church continued. Somewhere around 1925, the same year that Cora started teaching there, a missionary effort brought the Assembly to the village where it was housed in the Sanctified Church building that was joined by a boardwalk to the school building. Pastor Dave Adams from Westwego near New Orleans arrived via boat to serve the congregation. Tony Dufrene, brother of "Duffy", her landlord, preached at the church when Pastor Adams was not available.[4]

In Clarendon the Assembly Church was a two mile walk from the country home of Mattie Jones. The figures of two women made their way out of the dark block by the church where there were no sidewalks, past the W.W. Taylor place to Fourth Street where they could walk on continuous sidewalks down the hill toward town. Here, too, they would pick up the city street lights stationed at the end of every block, single bulbs covered by small metal enameled shades, forest green on top, glistening white underneath. By now it was after 8:00 o'clock and there were few vehicles on the roads. Half a mile away the sound of a racing motor rang out in the relative silence. Still ecstatic from the church service they made little note of it and walked on toward their destination. Along the way, in spontaneous harmony, their talented voices encored favorite chorus lines they sang earlier.

The taller and older of the women, Mrs. Jones, walked at a brisk pace for her age. Thirty years of farm work at the side of her husband on their truck farm had made her body lean and muscular. Miss Ferris, eighteen years younger, was also well conditioned for the physical exertion by the environmental challenges that existed in the rural communities where she had taught. Together she and Mrs. Jones had made this walk every Sunday since she came to live with her sister four years earlier. It was the same walk along the same route. At the end of Main Street they would cross the railroad tracks and follow the continuation of that street as it veered right through the sparsely populated white section across the track, near but apart from the compacted area known as colored town. North of the tracks the street lights dwindled out as the road approached the dump grounds just outside the city limits. From there they would turn west, connect with the narrow caliche topped Pampa highway and walk on to the lane to their home. Here their path was lighted only by the quarter moon in the eastern sky. [5]

▲ ▲ ▲

From where he was half a mile away, the wailing sounds of the church service were overwhelmed by sensual groans coming from the side of the road. He sat in the cab of a pickup with three white boys about his age as they waited their turn with the black girl in the bar ditch. He entertained them with boastings about his career as a procurer for the girls in a Chicago boarding house. They laughed, more at his slow and awkward way of talking than at the tales he was telling. They kept him talking with occasional sips from their pint of bootleg liquor. They laughed even more when his boasting had diverted his attention away from his business with the girl and she was able to slip away without paying him his fee. When he realized what had happened he bolted from the pickup in a fit of anger. The white boys roared off to finish the pint and to tease him by circling past him from time to time as he searched through the dump grounds for the girl and his fee. In their last circle their headlights briefly spotlighted the sisters as the black boy approached them from behind on the road beside the dump grounds. The flash of the headlights was just enough for all of them to view one another. The sight of the sisters sent the white boys back across the tracks for fear of being recognized by them. The ladies continued their walk as usual. For unknown reasons, the sight of the white women prompted the black boy to act.

He rushed on ahead and checked to be sure the pickup was gone and then turned back. He lashed out at the women with a sudden unexplained fury. Possibly venting the anger and insult he felt at being duped by the black girl and denied his fee from her, he raged. He held Cora by the throat in his left hand as he stunned Mrs. Jones with a blow to the head and battered her with a rock until she fell unconscious to the ground. He choked Cora until she could not speak. In a matter of minutes both women were in a state of unconsciousness. To assure control of both he dragged Mrs. Jones closer to her sister while he began his savage attack of Cora. At the peak of his sexual frenzy Mrs. Jones began to regain consciousness. He became aware that she was on her knees screaming and praying. Her frantic screams and melodic prayers added confusion to his frustrated attempts to rape. He suddenly forced an oral means to complete the act. Knowing they would be heard in nearby colored town, he silenced their screams with threats of death.

"Shut up that yelling or I'll kill you."

But then like a strange echo from his childhood upbringing, he helped the bloody, terrified ladies to their feet before he walked the 200 yards back to his room and calmly went to sleep. [6]

The bloody and hysterical women found their way to the home of a neighbor, Walter Green. His wife, Willie, gave them support and first aid while Walter ran to another neighbor, George Bulls, with the nearest telephone to alert the sheriff and call a doctor. From the moment Sheriff Guy Pierce took that call at 9:30 p.m. he knew he was dealing with an explosive situation.

Like the rape/murder case in Shamrock, a crime of this kind would enrage the citizenry and ignite the threat of mob retaliation. Pierce knew he had to take early command of this crime to prevent further tragedy in his district. Before he left to respond to the call, he deputized his wife, Mary, and assigned her the task of calling the Texas Rangers, the area DPS and the local American Legion. By the time the sheriff and the doctor climbed the steps onto the front porch that ran across the south side of the Green's house, a rapid community response to the tragedy was already in motion.[7]

This was a community that had never known such a threat to its safety. On this night the possibility of protection from an area and state-wide body of law enforcement was only two weeks old. The community naturally turned to its sheriff and to the American Legion. Emergency medical services in a hospital or emergency room were unknown. The personal attention of the doctor and his doctor bag met that need. Actually, Clarendon's country doctors were especially well enough trained and educated to merit the trust of their patients.

Mary Pierce was an experienced law official in her own right. Tonight as acting deputy sheriff she knew what to do and the urgency of doing it with dispatch.[8] In her first call to the night operator, Emma Ayers, she explained the nature of the emergency and listed for her priorities for the calls. In that time every telephone operator made all the emergency calls for her patrons. [9]

Emma weaved a cross stitch of telephone drops and jacks across her console as she contacted area crises manpower such as sheriff departments of nearby towns, doctors, DPS officers and the American Legion that served the community at that time as though it was a National

Guard unit. Mary and Emma worked as a team, Emma making the most of the limits to her 35 line switchboard, Mary utilizing time limits on the calls to explain the crime and the plan to rally the law enforcement team at the home of Walter Green.[10] Deputy Sheriff, Guy Wright, was one of those dispatched as a messenger to enlist those who had no telephone service by personal visits to their homes.[11]

Within an hour the nearly one hundred men began assembling at the Green place. Sheriff Pierce swore in the Legionnaires as posse and gave them his orders. The Highway Patrolmen sent the bulk of them out in teams of two and three in cars to patrol the county roads and to set up road blocks to all major roads coming into the area. All of these units were armed and several were accompanied by a Patrolman. They were to assure alarmed citizens that an army of men was in search of the suspect. Implicit in their presence was to send a message to potential lynch men that the highways and back roads of Donley County were under the command of armed men representing law and order.[12]

Other teams were sent on reconnaissance missions to the scene of the crime and on a house to house search through the black community. These calls were made in the same manner as Guy Wright's call to the Hunt home. In a calm but commanding tone the voice called out the name of the man of the house and then stated the purpose of the call. For the most part the Legionnaires were that well acquainted with the citizenry of colored town. All of the posse men had served in the armed services with military training and remembered its well defined procedures for taking command of a situation, for giving, receiving and executing orders without hesitation. By the time Texas Rangers Neal Arthur and Pat Taliaferro arrived in record time from Amarillo, the machinery of the law enforcement units were in place. Guy Perce and the Texas Rangers began their interrogation of the victims.[13]

The diverse group of human lives assembled at that moment of time and place in the living room of the Green home represented a sampling sweep through history. Rangers Arthur and Taliaferro, recently stationed in Amarillo as members of Homer Garrison's new breed of

Texas Rangers, brought with them their personal histories as vestiges of the older breed. Arthur initially joined the force as one of its first motor patrolmen. Taliaferro began as a deputy sheriff in Seymour and later Abilene before becoming a Ranger. His career was marked with flamboyant criminal investigations, high speed car chases and dramatic shoot outs.[14] While the father of Mrs. Jones and Miss Ferris was an orchard farmer much as Mrs. Jones' husband had been, he was also a law enforcement officer his entire adult life. He was first a U.S. Secret Agent and intermittently Texas Ranger and Deputy U. S. Marshall while he lived in Texas. He was a Deputy U. S. Marshall in the Oklahoma Territory and finally a deputy sheriff in Altus, Jackson County, Oklahoma after it became a state. Being the children of a lawman Mattie Lee and Cora saw their father bear the effects of gunshot wounds. From their older siblings they learned to endure fear for his safety during his long absences from home stoically, without speaking of it.[15]

Texas Rangers, Hugh Phares, Bob Crowder, B.M. ("Manny") Gault, Frank Mills, Neal Arthur, and Pat Taliaferro. Courtesy of Texas Ranger Hall of Fame, Waco, Texas.

The Ferris sisters were of sturdy stock, hard-working, independent and deeply religious, but tonight these ladies were wounded, bleeding and terrified. What they needed from the men who gathered around them was calming and a sense of security. They looked first to Guy Pierce because they knew him. He was completing his eighth year as a sheriff who kept things in order. But he had also grown up here; Mrs. Jones had known him since he was a child. Also unspoken were his World War I experiences. He had served aboard the USS Henderson, a troop ship that sailed through the torpedo infested waters of the North Sea to deliver American troops to France. Once he had been involved in a daring at sea evacuation of the 3000 troops aboard his ship when it caught on fire. There he had been a well- trained young sailor working as a member of his crew.[16] Tonight he was the man in charge of the law enforcement team responsible for the some 3000 lives of Donley County. Tonight his role in the interrogation was to calm the victims but defer the questioning to the Rangers because he knew that they had only recently been trained in the most up to date methods of interrogation. He also knew that what the ladies could tell them about the crime would be of the utmost importance to the case.

As Senior Investigating Officer, Ranger Arthur took the lead. He was a soft spoken man well trained in the polite social skills of a highway patrolman. His father's career was in the lumber business but his mother always maintained a boarding house in their home. He grew up with as many as eight or ten school teachers living in his home and sharing his family's meals. He identification with Miss Ferris as a school teacher and eased her into her account of the horrific attack.

The interrogation was an ordeal for the women. What had just happened to them was unimaginable. It is easy to assume that they had to undergo forensic examination of blood samples, tissue tears and cuts and examination of their clothing, but no mention of these things was ever made. If it happened, it was discreetly hidden from history. Having to talk about it to a man in the presence of other men was the limit of their endurance. Ranger Arthur mastered their hysteria with patience and their alliance with him as the kind of lawman their father was. He proceeded with his methodical questioning. By twelve-thirty when the Rangers and sheriff were called to the door by members of the posse, he had a well formed statement of the crime and a description of the assailant. Pierce excused himself and left with the posse man.

At the scene of the crime was a team headed up by Legionnaire Clyde Douglas, a local pharmacist. The persona he presented to his customers was the restrained, hardworking pharmacist who was in that corner of his store behind the counter or in the drug supply room behind it from sun to sun six days week. Known to only a few, Douglas had always had a penchant for exciting things. As a beginning pharmacy student at the University of Texas in 1917 he had been lured by the promises of quick involvement in frontline action made by the newly formed United States Army Ambulance Service. He volunteered and served in Italy where USAAS crews were known to have performed under the most demanding of conditions. He drove a motorized ambulance in Milan, Italy in the actual setting of Ernest Hemingway's *Farewell to Arms*. After the war he completed pharmacy school in Dallas with plans to return to Clarendon. The night that he arrived in Clarendon on the evening train he came upon an armed robbery in progress at the train station. On foot he gave chase to the robber and made a citizen's arrest. After the sheriff took over his prisoner, Douglas rendered aid to the elderly victim of the robbery.[17]

On this night he quickly discovered unusual footprints left in the blow sand still damp from a rain shower earlier in the day. The tracks led from the dump grounds 200 yards back to colored town. With a flashlight, sometimes on his hands and knees, he followed the prints with a pattern of crosses in the heel print to a shanty at the north end of Jefferson Street. It was the home of Albert Boyd, most often known as Marble Eye, Kingfish of the colored town bootleggers.[18]

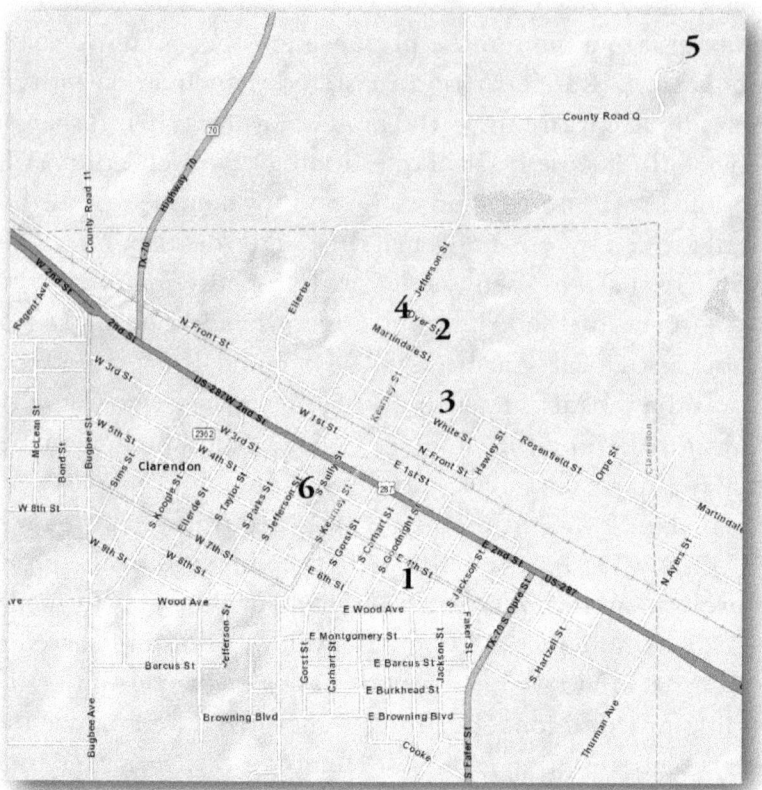

1. Assembly of God Church; 2. Scene of the attack; 3. Walter Green's house; 4. Marble Eye Boyd's house; 5. The Ferris sisters' home; 6. Donley County Courthouse and Downtown Clarendon.

Douglas and his team entered the house at roughly 12:30 a.m. and they found three young black men sleeping in a bedroom at the back of the house. Two were easily awakened and co-operated with questions directed at them by the posse men, though they appeared nervous in doing so. They identified themselves as local cotton pickers in town for the weekend. They indicated that the other man was a fellow worker. The third man was sleeping more soundly but when he was finally awakened gave little more information than his name. At this point Douglas and his team found no evidence in the room to link men to the tracks that had led the posse men to this house, but the behavior of the men raised suspicion. This was reported to Guy Pierce and the Texas Rangers as they were winding up the interrogation of the victims at the Green place. After conferring with Douglas and viewing the tracks, they made their first contact with the three young men. As lawmen they sensed that they had enough probable cause evidence to make an arrest, but in this situation the lawmen knew they needed to cover their bases to the letter of the law. They opted to seek a search warrant before making the arrest.[19]

County Judge, R. Y. King, was called out to hear the evidence and issue a warrant. The month before, King and his wife had adopted infants, twin girls, so tiny they needed to be fed every two hours through the night. Mr. King was already up, so he wasted no time in arriving at his office. [20]

County Judge R. Y. King was called out to issue the warrant for Norman's arrest and later took his confession. Shown with his wife Lulu. Photo courtesy of the King family.

When they returned with the warrant around 2:00 a.m. the Sheriff and the Rangers easily found a pair of shoes under the bed of the third young man whose heels matched the distinctive footprint found at the scene of the crime. All three of the young black men identified the boots as belonging to Morris Norman. They were a part of his uniform issue with the Civilian Conservation Corp from which he had been discharged the month before in Durand, Illinois.[21] Morris Norman had only been in the Clarendon area for one week.[22]

By 2:30 a.m. he had been arrested and taken in the patrol car of the Rangers to the dump ground where he was held and interrogated. At first he denied that he had perpetrated the crime but when confronted with details of the assault obtained by the investigation team from the victims, he began to admit his guilt. Investigator, Ranger Arthur, pressed him for details. Under this pressure he confessed, giving an account remarkably similar to the story told by the victims.[23] Within his story the lawmen also spotted Norman's most prominent point of vulnerability – a longing for his mother. The investigative format used by the Rangers was one incorporated by the newly formed Texas Bureau of Investigation to ferret out criminal patterns. It was the genesis of those formats currently used by investigative profilers. Suspects were asked for information about their families. Even then, the forensic investigator recognized the family of origin issues that correlated with the development of criminality.[24]

As this interrogation was in progress rumblings of the crime circulated in the community. The sheriff was receiving reports of threats to assemble a counter posse, a lynch mob, to avenge it. He and his Deputies circulated in the colored town giving advice to these citizens on how to keep a low profile and how to protect themselves. The Highway Patrolmen and American Legion posse men tightened their efforts to seal off colored town.[25]

*Picture taken from two blocks east of the Assembly of God Church in
1938, showing the scene of the crime, Walter Green's home and home
of the victims in the background. Photo by Ernest L. Hunt, 1938.*

The investigating officers took him to the Walter Green home to be
identified by the victims. Upon seeing Norman again they became hysterical. Having to look at him and pressed to verify with certainty that
he was their assailant, they were terrified. This was a second rape. As
Norman rushed to the side of one of them offering his apologies, their
anxiety accelerated to a point of shock. Norman had provided his own
identification. The officers quickly removed him from the scene. [26]

Sometime after 4:00 a.m. County Judge, R. Y. King, already in his
office from issuing the warrant, met with Norman and the officers to
type up the confession from his statement to the Rangers. Seated before his Underwood typewriter King began this tedious task. The topics
covered in the statement were crude and distasteful. Norman's use of
language was limited, at times barely coherent, and at times strongly
flavored with unfamiliar Chicago street talk. A verbatim version of his
confession would require a translation in any setting. The words that
King pecked out on his Underwood had to represent the truth of what

his statement to the Rangers regarding his acts at the dump ground had been, written in language that could be presented to a jury. At 5:30 a.m. on October 31, 1938, Morris Norman signed the confession. Immediately Sheriff Pierce and the Rangers took their prisoner/suspect to a jail cell in Amarillo some sixty miles away.

Meantime rumblings about forming a mob to avenge the crime were already being heard at the courthouse.[27] These for Mr. King were stark reminders of the times in Hedley when he lived with death threats for defending a black man. Prompted by the lessons learned from the 1930 riots, Pierce knew that time was of the essence.

The first call that Mary Pierce had made as her husband left for the scene of the crime had been to the Amarillo Police Headquarters. From there the alarm was spread. A part of that first response was to alert the *Amarillo Daily News* office.[28] The staff was already there in force to cover the calls generated by the *War of the Worlds* broadcast. A reporter was quickly dispatched to Clarendon. He met with Mrs. Pierce at the jail. She was able to relay first reports from the law officers on the scene about the nature and location of the crime, the identity of the victims and a description of the assailant. By the time the reporter left for Amarillo to file his story, Norman had been apprehended but the official arrest had not yet been made. As Pierce and the Rangers arrived at the Amarillo jail with their prisoner the *Amarillo Daily News'* account of the story was reaching citizens all over the Panhandle. Bold headlines read:

NEGRO SOUGHT IN CLARENDON ATTACK
Donley Aroused As Two Women Are Assaulted [29]

People in the Panhandle of Texas had a real and serious problem to deal with. For some time now they had been kept on edge with daily reports about the rumblings of war in Europe but now for the first time in nearly a decade, the eminent threat of mob violence was smoldering in their midst.

As the work day began in Clarendon, District Attorney, John M. Deaver, lost no time in spurring the district judicial system into action. In 1930 during the Shamrock/Wellington affair he was serving as Hall County Judge only thirty miles away. He was well acquainted with the dilemmas faced by his colleague, Collingsworth County Judge Gribble, because of the hesitancy of his system to act in the first few hours after the crime. With the charges against Norman filed, Deaver's first move was to appeal to District Judge A. S. Moss on this last day of October to reconvene the October Grand Jury. By the end of the day on Monday Moss had signed the order to reconvene the Grand Jury for Wednesday. November 2, 1938.

The November 1st edition of the Amarillo Daily News ran the headlines:

DONLEY GRAND JURY IS CALLED IN ATTACK CASE

The article quoted the officers with details of the crime as well as their eye witness account of the assailant's behavior while in custody. This statement to the press seemed to be addressing lessons learned from the Shamrock/Wellington case. In that case white citizens of Shamrock had been infuriated by the way the Rangers had made such a show of protecting the black murderer while those standing up for the violated woman had not been duly avenged. The press message on November 1, 1938 emphasized that being brought to a speedy and just trial to defend the honor of ravished womanhood was a "smug, pretentious, cold blooded assailant with an ebony hued face." Officers were quoted as saying that this attack was one of the most brutal ever recorded in the South. The second message was that every precaution would be taken to prevent mob violence.[30]

One of the Rangers, presumably Pat Talafierro, had allowed himself to be interviewed by the Press to describe the arrest, the scene in County Judge King's office, the trip from Clarendon to Amarillo, and even details of the confession. Taliaferro had a history, as a deputy sheriff and later Texas Ranger in Abilene, of using newspaper headlines to promote his agenda. With the Norman case he was using this finesse to manage public opinion.

In any regard, management of press releases was of vital importance. If such a thing was possible, input into the rumor mill could be used to

advantage. In the Sherman affair as in the Shamrock case, irrespon-
sibility with the local press had contributed significantly to the rumor
mill and to the unrest of the mobs. In Sherman it was rumored that the
Governor had ordered the Rangers not to fire. This had emboldened
the mob to push into the court house. In the Honey Grove lynching the
first gathering of people had been members of the press there to witness
the arrest of the murderer.[31] In Clarendon under the management of
a more polished law enforcement team, there seemed to be an effort to
"tell the press before the press told." [32] At the same level official input
was fed into the rumor mill. Among "private sources" it was known that
snipers were in place on the upper floor of the jail and armed lawmen
in plain clothes were securing every public gathering.[33]

On November 2nd the Grand Jury reassembled. Upon completing
the investigation of the matter of Morris Norman's attacks upon the
persons of Mattie Jones and Miss Cora Ferris, Edwin Baley, Foreman, reported that the Grand Jury returned to the Court one bill of indictment
which was received by the Court and ordered filed as The State of Texas
vs. - - - - No. 1972, a Felony. The next day, it was stated in the *Amarillo
Daily News*, that Sheriff Pierce served Norman with the indictment in his
Amarillo jail cell. Court records for November 5, 1938 stated that Morris
Norman, the defendant, was brought before the Court for arraignment
and having no counsel was appointed counsel, W. T. Link, J. R. Porter
and John Knorpp, local attorneys, to defend him.[34] It is uncertain if that
court appearance was actual or de facto in order to protect his safety.
In a statement to the Amarillo reporter Sheriff Pierce promised that
Norman would be kept in the Amarillo jail until the trial.

The Grand Jury was dismissed. On that day further actions of the
Court were to order that a special venire of 50 jurymen be summoned
by the Sheriff to report on November 8, 1938 at 9:00 a.m. for the trial of
Cause No. 1972.[35]

In reporting on this indictment, the November 3rd edition of the
Amarillo Daily News quoted Miss Cora Ferris' statement to the Grand Jury
that she had been criminally attacked and inhumanly abused by Morris
Norman. Cause No. 1972 was for this assault. Mrs. Jones was said to have

testified to the Grand Jury that she was attacked and battered about the face and head with a rock. The Grand Jury took no action on this allegation. District Attorney, John Deaver, was quoted by the *Amarillo Daily News* as saying he would seek the death penalty. The rest of the article was devoted to the matter of community outrage at the crime and threats of mob violence. Security measures to prevent this were carefully detailed. [36]

Press coverage in the *Donley County Leader* was more impassioned. An editorial license to vilify the accused and to use racially biased language was freely used. Norman was described as "20 - year old smug, pretentious, Illinois Negro in a jail cell in Amarillo." The Ranger's phrase, "termed the most brutal attack in the history of the southland," was repeated as was the phrase, "Norman, with no show of remorse on his ebony hued face, signed a lurid written confession before officers." It appeared that editor J. C. Estlack had obtained actual access to Norman's confession. He published details and even direct quotes from the confession. Direct quotes from the victims about their testimony before the Grand Jury were also published. The Texas Ranger's public opinion campaign was well represented by the *Donley County Leader's* news story. And nowhere the cause more clearly stated and the fundamental heartbeat of the law abiding citizens of Donley County more eloquently represented than in Editor J. C. Estlack's "Temple of Truth" editorial entitled "Brutes in Human Form."

BRUTES IN HUMAN FORM

▲ ▲ ▲

An Editorial

"Man-made laws do not always prevent crime, but they do provide a penalty. Compliance with our laws in Donley County in the past has established a reputation for this section of a high order of citizenship. Very wisely our lawmakers provided the supreme penalty for certain crimes. The screams of ravished womanhood sounds the death knell for the brute in human form – by law. The stamina and strength of character of a Donley county jury may be depended upon to mete justice to the malefactor. In this dark hour when men's souls are being tried under stress of resentment, the orderly process of law is deemed best. Wisdom, valor, character and other Godly graces go into the melting pot of public opinion. Donley County's citizenship fully realizes that our laws must be upheld. If this brutal wrong could have been righted by human hands, that act would have been accomplished Sunday night. But it can't. It is never too late to mete justice to the transgressor. And that shall be done with swift justice."[37]

The editorial sanctioned and in fact, pled for the death penalty within the orderly process of law. It affirmed the matter of moral conviction and strength of character inherent in the execution of justice under the stress of such resentment and declared certainty that this justice would be swift. Also it validated for the many southerners in the Clarendon area and to the fifteen ladies in Shamrock that the matter of defense of the virtue of womanhood was being proclaimed.[38]

With a singleness of purpose Donley County and officials of the 100th Judicial District prepared for the trial of Morris Norman just nine days after he committed the crime. Determined to prevent the mistakes of the 1930 season of riots was a well-organized body of law enforcement officers. In the November 3rd edition of the *Amarillo Daily News* Sheriff Pierce was quoted as saying:

"I never saw so much response by any group of officers to that given my call for aid last Sunday night. The officers arrived in a surprisingly short time and it was this whole-hearted cooperation that brought the quick arrest and confession." [39]

6

On Main Street

THE MORNING TRAIN from Amarillo greeted Monday's first light as it spilled onto Clarendon's main street.[1] One of the canvass mail sacks tossed from the open door of the mail car onto the waiting depot wagon manned by Andy Robertson contained the rolled copies of the *Amarillo Daily News* addressed to its Clarendon subscribers. Behind the mail car, packages from the baggage car were hand placed onto the shiny bright green Railway Express cart in the hands of Express Agent, Walter Green. Weary from the night-long ordeal that played out in his home only hours before, Mr. Green was at his station as always. This morning his hastily donned Railway Express uniform jacket and cap covered yesterday's crumpled cloths and distracted from his day old beard.

As the water spout started swinging back into place alongside the wooden water tower, a loud hiss from the engine signaled its preparation for departure. Doors to the mail and baggage cars rolled shut and down the line the Conductor, in navy blue uniform and standing on a boarding step, leaned away from the door to wave his signal to the Engineer that all passengers were safely aboard. A loud whistle pierced the air and the drive shaft nudged the engine's wheels forward. Within minutes the train disappeared into the bright orange of the rising sun.

View of main street Clarendon and a Fourth of July
Parade, circa 1943. Photo by Ernest L. Hunt.

Holding the long green tongue of the Railway Express wagon Mr.
Green pulled his cargo away from the tracks. In the quiet that followed
the departed train, the vibrato clack of the large wooden spoked wheels
sounded a morning prelude to the day as they rolled over the brick pave-
ment toward the express office on the west end of the station. Andy
loaded the mail sacks into his car and headed to the alley door of the
Post Office down the street. By the time that the Post Office windows
opened at 8:00 a.m. the bold headlines on the front page of the *Amarillo
Daily News* awaited its readers.

Patrons with half unfolded papers in hand joined the clusters of
two or three men already assembled along the high soda fountain bar
at Legionnaire Clyde Douglas' Drug Store and the long table height bar
at Legionnaire F.E. Caraways Café on the north block. Today the usual
morning coffee-talk was already centered on the rumors about the events
of the previous night. Though these and several others of the players
in the Clarendon main street morning scene were also Legionnaires
and members of the posse the night before, they had been sworn to secrecy and at least publicly honored that pledge. Clyde Douglas stayed in
the pharmacy room behind the counter with the door closed. Caraway

worked in the kitchen of his café avoiding the customers as they discussed the rumors and compared them to the news article.

The paper described the crime in vague terms. The moral decorum of that time dictated that the words used to discuss such things were whispered and in the presence of woman and children, they were banned. Even the whispering men had no words for the "lurid acts" they had heard about. They did have words for a range of opinions regarding justice for the acts. By morning coffee time it was already known that the assailant had been captured and was secured in an Amarillo jail. All day fresh rumors were generated by the flurry of activity at the Court House

Unnoticed on Main Street was the early morning activity surrounding the victims who remained at the Green home. By daybreak word of the tragedy had reached their fellow church members and they quietly attended to their needs. One took them into her home in a nearby village where they could begin their recovery in seclusion. Neighbors fed Mrs. Jones' livestock and milked her cows. Men of the congregation monitored for any unusual traffic on the sole access to their home, the single lane winding eastward uphill off of Highway 18. Within the city limits the highway was Jefferson Street, the main street of colored town, the north end of which was some 200 yards west of the dump ground. That site was in the care of area lawmen.

By that afternoon rumors coming out of the Court House revealed that the Grand Jury had been reconvened for Wednesday morning. The rumor mill was hard pressed to keep pace with the rapid movement of the local justice system and the presence of area news reporters. More discreet but ominously present were the rumors seeping out of the pockets of Klan thinking that were scattered throughout the county.

As evening approached the focus of attention shifted away to other things. Main street routines went on as usual. Storekeepers tidied their stores for the next day, turned on a single bulb night light and left for home. The bell-like clinking of the flag being lowered in front of the Post Office punctuated the quiet descending over the main street. The flag was gathered into the arms of the clerk, reverently folded into a triangle and placed in the drawer assigned for it at the Post Master's desk.

It was Halloween and the school children would attend the annual Halloween Carnival there. Each classroom teacher would compete for the best decorations and scary tricks and games. Miss Steven's second grade room, as always, put on a spectacular show. She was known for her large collection of theme classroom decorations. Halloween represented one of her best collections. Black and orange construction paper witches, spiders, bats on wing and black cats covered the walls and dangled from the ceiling. In the back of the room was her specialty, the chamber of horror table. Parents contributed the time and effort involved in preparing her recipes. There were peeled grapes for eyes, spaghetti and catsup for "guts." Miss Stevens added in dried corn kernels for teeth and horses tail clippings for witches' hair. Adults coaxed the children to "feel" the gruesome articles and laughed to see them shiver, squeal and run away. They preferred bobbing for apples, hearing "spooks stories" read by Miss Stevens and smearing their faces with the sticky residue of black licorice sticks, candy corn and the thick orange icing that adorned the cookies. After a scant two hours of Halloween trickery and simulated horror the children retuned home with their parents.

By half-past seven few lights remained on in the store buildings along the main street. One glowed dimly through the front widow from the light still on in the mail workroom in the back of the Post Office building. Ernest Hunt was completing the final sort of all westbound mail for the day. Standing in front of the large pigeon-hole sort desk he gathered a bundle of mail from each hole, attached a routing slip and wrapped it around each bundle with burlap twine which he cut from the spool with a deft undercut from his pocket knife. This task finished, he gathered the bundles onto a rolling table and made his way to the canvass mail bags that were hanging mouth open on a large partitioned metal rack. Adjusting the angle of his head to read the routing slip through his bifocal eye glasses, he picked up each bundle and tossed it into the appropriate mailbag. Interrupting this process was a loud knock on the back door announcing the arrival of Andy Robertson. Hunt removed the large bundle of keys hanging from a belt loop to his khaki pants and fingered through them for that door key on his way there.

Both men stood beside the mail sacks as Hunt officially closed off each bag by pulling the draw string shut and attaching a pad lock to a fastener at the closed mouth of the bag. He briskly handed the bags to Andy who grasped them and held them against his body with his crippled arm until he had all he could hold onto. Hunt carried the others as they rushed for Andy's car parked in the alley. The train was due in ten minutes.

As it topped Bugee Hill and left Clarendon, the whistle of the evening train signaled the closing of another day. Locking the front door to the Post Office lobby behind him, he left for home in the Franklin car parked at the main street entrance. On the way there his headlights shone in passing onto the several unfamiliar vehicles that were quietly circulating through the streets of Clarendon and on to back roads throughout the county. He knew with assurance the pre-established checkpoints maintaining an invisible cordon around colored town to seal it away from any of the real horrors that might be lurking in the shadows of that Halloween night.

7

The Cast

THE TRIAL DATE was set for November 8. It would be staged in the Courtroom on the second floor of the historic Donley County Court House. The calling of the special session of the Grand Jury the day after the crime prompted the need to prepare the public for what was coming. Plans to secure the court house were being released to the press. This was soon after the entire third floor of the original building had been removed and this would affect the way the security plans were carried out. The third story towers over the stairwells had provided the advantage of better lookouts and more control of access to the courtroom. This security now had to be contained within the courtroom itself. The trial was set, ground rules were clearly stated. Attendance to the trial would be limited to adults who would be searched before entering the courtroom. The doors would be locked as soon as the seats were filled. All entrances to the courtroom and to the court house would be guarded.[1]

Complicating the trial security, November 8, was also general election day and this was the day that W. Lee O'Daniel would be elected Governor of Texas.[2] On the one hand this could attract the older voters who were his most enthusiastic fans because of his campaign promises to create old age pensions and other benefits for the elderly. More "grey coats," or avid champions of the Southern beliefs, might be in town and in the Court House casting their votes in polling places on the first floor. On the other hand, election laws prohibiting loitering within 100 yards of the polls could be utilized to add strength to the efforts of the lawmen to maintain crowd control.

Donley County Courthouse as it appeared in 1939. Photo courtesy TXDoT.

Key players were preparing to play their parts in the saga that would unfold on November 8. Each man came to the scene with his unique personality and range of experiences that would qualify him to move the team effort toward their common goal.

A leader in the cast was District Attorney, John M. Deaver. First elected to this office in 1932 he was known throughout the state as a prosecutor with one of the highest records of convictions. In the Panhandle he was active as a Mason, member of the American Legion and in his church and its area governing body, the Presbytery. And he was a Democrat, not only as a candidate, but as a party member promoting its causes. With all of these serious accomplishments he was noted for his sense of humor.[3]

In Hall County, his home county, every election was preceded by a series of political rallies staged in the various small communities throughout the county. The rally format was a hearty meal followed by spirited debates among the candidates in the form of campaign speeches. Deaver was innately endowed with the talents of a standup comedian and talk show host. He knew how to play to the crowd. In one of his campaigns his chief opponent was not so endowed. He had only one speech that he recited almost verbatim at every rally. During their first debate Deaver spotted this weakness and capitalized upon it. He signaled to his secretary to take down the speech in shorthand and subsequently he memorized it. After that he would ask permission from the rally host to go first with his speech, the memorized speech of his opponent. This left the other candidate speechless.[4]

District Attorney of the 100ᵗʰ Judicial District, John M. Deaver (1898 – 1978). Photo courtesy of John M. Deaver, II.

In his personal life he was the eldest son of prominent pioneer at-torney and banker, Judge Houston E. Deaver. To his family and later to his country he was a hero. As a young adolescent he once accompanied his mother and three younger sisters on a trip toward Clarendon in their Dodge touring car. As they passed through the town of Lelia Lake and beside the lake of that name, a flash flood sent a torrent of water racing across the highway that quickly inundated the car. Deaver was able to free himself and by tearing through the canvass top of the car, to release his mother so that she could swim safely to shore. He swam to shore with one of his sisters but was unable to return fast enough to save the other two.[5]

As an older teen he interrupted his studies at Trinity University in San Antonio to join the armed services in 1917. He served with the Marines Sixth, Second Army Division. By the last days of that war he had attained the rank of Lieutenant. In the Meuse-Argonne campaign the men he commanded were responsible for building pontoon bridges across the river Aisne in the Allies final effort to push the Germans out of France. The mission was extremely dangerous, the casualties were high and the men on both sides of the river were exhausted. Rumors of the Armistice were circulating with increasing certainty, yet orders from the higher command pushed the battle plans. Young Lt. Deaver, not yet voting age, viewed the situation in all its complexities and took a chance on delaying his orders to push his men into the deadly river mission. At 11:00 a.m. on November 11, 1918 the quiet that swept across France rewarded his concern for the lives of those under his command. This is the man that would perform the role of prosecutor. His goal was to execute justice swiftly enough to placate the cry for vengeance, statutory enough to satisfy the law and low key enough to maintain control of the situation.[6]

Commanding the bench was District Judge A. S. Moss whose le-gal career had now entered its fourth decade. He was characterized by decorum in his courtroom and in his person. In any assembly he could be distinguished by his round black horn-rimmed glasses and his split-tailed coat. In his private practice he was the law partner of Deaver. In his political life he was concluding his second year as District Judge of the 100th Judicial District. His personal cause had been the founding and support of the Texas State Bar Association where he represented the movement to raise and maintain high ethical standards for the practice of law. These were lofty standards that attributed to the lawyer the responsibility for upholding the constitutional right of all people, including minorities, while keeping in balance those rights protecting against misuse of power, and for taking a stand regarding the deficiencies in protecting the public against the menace of crime. Cause No. 1972 would present a special challenge for him to respond to the public cry for swift action without compromising fair trial standards.[7]

John Ralph "J.R." Porter (1893-1956)
Attorney since 1927, Civic Leader and
member of Norman's defense team.

In defending Morris Norman Judge Porter's mission was not an easy one. First, he had to consolidate the defense team, the entire bar of Clarendon. The reasoning behind appointing every practicing lawyer in town to defend the accused man is uncertain though it might have been to spare any defense attorney from being the sole target of Klan threats as Judge King had been. Additional confusion about this matter was that up to the day of the trial, Clarendon street gossip maintained that Dusty Miller, prominent trial lawyer from Amarillo, had been appointed to defend Norman. What is certain is that Clarendon's three lawyers were involved, under order, in a single mission and it was a delicate one. It was in a time and place where, however benign or malignant, racism existed. The community was outraged and fearful that this would explode into mob violence. It was a case of unimaginable brutality with a confession that matched the victim's account of it. How could one rise to the defense of such a man accused of such a crime without inflammatory consequences? [8]

William Thomas "W.T." Link, (1885-1969) Photo by Ernest L. Hunt, circa 1940. Link was a practicing attorney since 1911 and a member of Norman's defense team.

W. T. Link was the elder member of the team. His practice of law had spanned nearly three decades from time as County Attorney to the practice of civil law, which he preferred because his experiences with criminal law had soured him on those people. Before coming to Clarendon he had served four years in the U. S. Navy during the Presidency of Teddy Roosevelt.[9] Judge Link was known to have been a stickler for details and unyielding when he was convinced he was right. During one trial he had engaged the opposing attorney in an argument over a point of law to such an extent that the Judge ordered a recess and instructed both attorneys that if they did not return with the matter settled he would hold them both in contempt. [10]

John Knorpp, age 22, was the third member of the defense team. He had just completed law school and was excited to be included on the team. While his personal mission was to learn from the experience, his role with the defense counsel had a stabilizing influence upon the public. Knorpp descended from two of the most respected pioneer families in the community. [11]

John C. Knorpp, (1911 – 1999) Gained his
first trial experience as a member of Norman's
defense team. Photo courtesy of the family.

Minor characters in the cast were members of the press though, as fate would have it, their contribution would leave to history the most accurate accounting of the whole affair from beginning to end.

J. C. Estlack, owner, publisher, editor and chief reporter of the *Donley County Leader* was no doubt on the scene at the sheriff's office and court house as soon as the alarm was sounded. Since his paper was published on Thursdays only, he did not break the story. But in the November 3rd edition of his paper he uniquely represented the thinking and feelings of the community caught up in the drama. His rhetoric was impassioned and inflammatory but he spelled out the issues at stake.

There was subtle reference in Estlack's editorial to another such time in Donley County when the death penalty was ordered in a trial in the same courtroom in an era when the laws dictated that it be carried out in the same legal jurisdiction in the form of hanging. The way in which this case had been sensationalized by outside press, the Paparazzi of that day, had offended the local citizenry. This was especially true in the way that it caused the local sheriff to be characterized as a hangman. This unspoken history underlined Estlack's emphasis on the duties of law and order. At the trial Estlack would write his own eye witness account and this would be unique.[12]

Covering the trial for the *Amarillo Daily News* was its publisher, Gene Howe, better known as Old Tack after his folksy daily column, "The Tactless Texas." As a businessman and promoter of those interests in the Panhandle, he was known as "Mr. Panhandle, Amarillo's one-man Chamber of Commerce." [13] He counted District Attorney, John Deaver, among his personal friends.

Vital to the trial was the selection and summons of fifty men to be the special venire of jurors. This duty fell to Sheriff Guy Pierce. The Judge's order had given him three days to complete this task and return the list to the County Clerk. A statutory requirement of the capital offense special venire was that the defendant or his attorneys have the jury list at least two full days prior to the trial. Under the statute he was also bound to "summons persons of good character who can read and write and are not prejudiced against the defendant or biased in his favor." This was much for him to consider. [14] With such strong community sentiments in favor of "a peculiar chivalry"[15] for the victims of the crime, care had to be taken lest he be liable for selecting "a hangman's jury." At least two of the rural communities in Donley County had the reputation of being more racially biased, one even rumored to have carried out a secret lynching and others guilty of some near death beatings. These communities needed to be included in the juror list but included in balance. Sheriff Guy Pierce who was personally acquainted with the people of his community knew "Donley County shoes." This would be factored in his selection of the special venire. [16]

The matter of bias because of publicity was harder to determine in that time. Mass media consisted of a weekly local paper, a daily Amarillo paper and the radio. The papers were for the most part delivered by mail. The 1930 census count of Donley County households that owned a radio was roughly 38%.[17] Radio ownership was more infrequent in the rural communities, and those famers who included reading a newspaper in their daily routine is also assumed to be low. Farmers were more isolated from the places where people gathered to talk and pass on rumors but they also seemed to have a very active word of mouth communication system. Since the highly respected victims were farmers, loading the jurors list with farmers was a bias in favor of the prosecution but difficult to avoid due to the high percentage of famers in Donley County.

Hidden factors that can only be assumed to have played a part in the makeup of the venire were age and armed service history. The mean age of the jury panel turned out to be 45.[18] Pierce's rationale for this is limited to speculation. Perhaps it was a way of eliminating the "grey coat" factor or maybe in his opinion younger men had better judgment and were more likely to exercise it expeditiously. Since the American Legion had been called out as a body to form the posse that tracked down the suspect it was necessary that veterans be excluded from this list.

No blacks would be on the list. Though they were citizens and had the duty/right to vote and to jury service no black had ever been in a jury pool in Donley County. Most would have been disqualified because they were not registered to vote or were illiterate. But in that time the use of pre-emptory challenge to exclude black jurors was common across the nation. In this case it was also unsafe for any black citizen to be outside of their section north of the railroad tracks.

In 1938 women did not even have the right to serve on a jury in Texas. The 21st Amendment that gave them the right to vote left the matter of jury service up to the States. It was not until 1954 that the Texas Constitution was amended to grant women this right and not until 1979 that the use of pre-emptory challenge to exclude minorities and women from jury service was prohibited by the Supreme Court.[19] Morris Norman would be tried before an all white, all male jury.

The matter of summons was a special issue with this venire. Depending on mail service within the limited time frame was not feasible. This was a jury panel that must report timely and in numbers that assured a speedy jury selection. The statute actually stated a venire "of no less than fifty men." [20] The sheriff and his deputies had to deliver each summons personally and were hard pressed to complete a summons of fifty men. The morning of the trial 37 men selected as the Special Venire presented themselves to the court. [21]

Other provisions of the Special Venire Act were to grant the judge the power to draw jurors from the established jury pool in the event that a full jury was not selected from the Special Venire. He covered all bases. On November 7th Judge Moss had appointed a jury commission to select juries for the next term of the court. He had this pool to draw from if need be. [22]

An unknown number of unidentified men provided the safety net for the whole effort of carrying out this trial. These were the state and area lawmen that had been actively involved in suppressing and preventing any mob activity since the night of the crime and were now preparing to be in place at the trial. At least thirty of these officers would be in and around the courthouse on the day of the trial. It is intriguing to speculate about how this effort was organized and implemented. Communication among the men on the scene was without any of the electronic devises available today. For example, an officer manning the main staircase 2nd floor landing overlooking the south court house lawn could not use a radio or cell phone to alert the sniper positioned in the second floor of the jail house that a group of men was headed north toward the jail. Men in any of the court house positions, east and west entrances, front and rear staircases, outlooks in the second floor east and south towers and those securing the second floor hallways, would have to act independently within their stations. No doubt there had been briefings ahead of time but their true unity rested in oneness of purpose. [23]

Only eight years earlier what had happened in Sherman, Honey Grove and nearby Wellington and Shamrock in the spring and summer of 1930 was the strongest motivator for what they would not allow to happen. All of these incidents had been provoked by irreprehensible crimes committed by black assailants on white victims but it was the barbarity of the white mobs that had been the most brutish and shameful legacy in the history of Texas. [24]

The Sherman incident bore a striking similarity to the Clarendon case. The 1930 cases had horrified law abiding citizens of Texas. They had served as both embarrassment and inspiration to the law enforcement community. In Donley County the citizenry and the law enforcement communities were committed to the goal of upholding a higher standard. Among the area DPS and law enforcement personnel on the scene in Clarendon there were no doubt those who had firsthand experience with the Wellington/Shamrock case. They knew their script and they knew the cues in the production that would play out next Tuesday, November 8, in the 100th Judicial District courtroom.

8

The Trial

*The mettle of any community of men is forged upon the anvil
at hand, and tempered in the crucible of time.*

AUTHOR

IT WAS ELECTION Day and the polls on the first floor of the courthouse
had opened at 7:00 a.m., two hours before the trial was scheduled to
begin. Statewide this election was not expected to attract much attention because W. Lee "Pappy" O'Daniel had won a landslide victory in the
primary election and even though he had a minor party opponent, in
that time a victory as the Democratic Party candidate was tantamount
to victory in the November election. Ironically, the only issue offered on
the ballot was a constitutional amendment abolishing the requirement
of candidates for public office to sign an oath that they would refrain
from dueling while in office.[1] While a low voter turnout was anticipated,
the election did provide an excuse to be at the courthouse and any reason for a crowd to gather and linger was an opportunity for the feelings
of the populace about the crime to ignite the mob spirit.

With respect for this, every movement of any of the players involved in the trial would be calculated to be low key, punctual and restricted to the area of his station or duty. Officers of the law stationed themselves at each of the entrances and exits to the jail and courthouse and along the roadways through which the defendant would travel to and from the trial. They were conspicuously armed with their appropriate service weapons. The judge and attorneys accompanied by Court Bailiffs quickly entered the courthouse through the west entrance and its internal staircase.

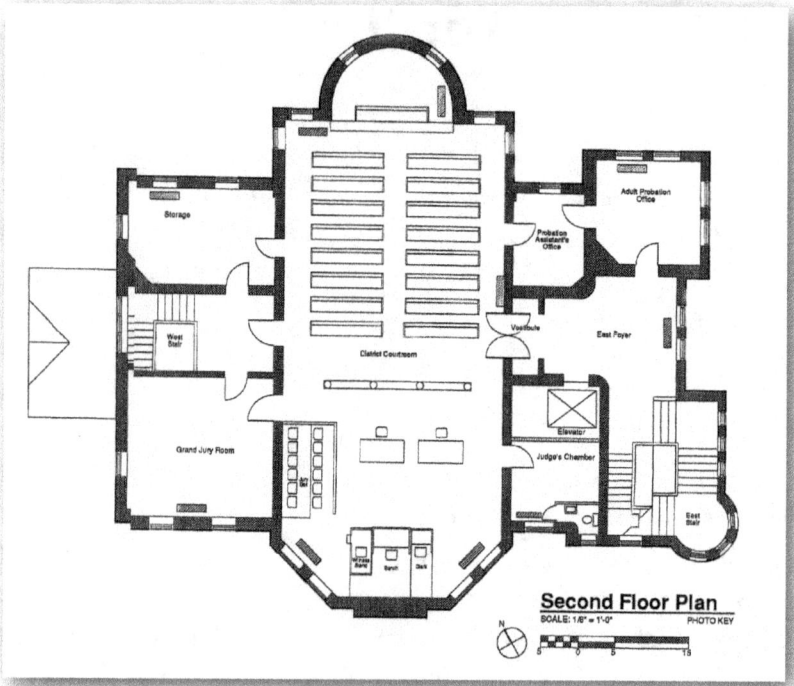

Donley County Courthouse second floor layout.

Timed to arrive after the security officers were in place and the judge and attorneys for the prosecution and defense were waiting in their designated areas, the defendant arrived by motor car from Amarillo. He was accompanied by Potter County Sheriff Adams, Donley County Sheriff Pierce and Texas Rangers, Arthur and Taliaferro. To move him quickly through the west entrance and up that staircase he was hand-cuffed but did not wear ankle chains.   He joined his defense attorneys in the northwest room off of the west foyer to the courtroom.

By 8:00 a.m. some of the men of the special venire began arriving. The Bailiff and security lawmen searched them and checked their names against the list.   The urgency of their compliance with sum-mons had been communicated at the time they were served but today time was the essence in all matters pertaining to the trial.   There was some anxiety about the venire showing up in numbers sufficient to as-sure an early selection of the jury.   By the time they were seated in the courtroom to prepare for voir dire 37 men had reported for duty. [2]

100th Judicial District Courtroom on the second floor of the Donlry County Courthouse. Photo by Nita L. Dyslin 2013.

Spectators had also arrived early to assure that they would be admitted to the courtroom. It had been made clear in advance that all spectators would be searched and admitted only as long as there was seating for them. Children were not allowed. Few women were present. Social mores of that time dictated that words they would hear spoken in the trial were not meant for the ears of ladies. The women present were likely close friends of the victims and were there to support them through the ordeal of having to speak such words.

Reporters of the area newspapers assembled prepared to take meticulous notes. To date their coverage of the story had been an essential factor in preparing the public for what would be expected of them during the trial. Members of the press were personally invested in its outcome.

At 9:00 a.m. the trial began. The special venire was assembled and seated. The spectators filled the remainder of the courtroom seating. The doors to the courtroom were locked and guarded by law officers. The District Attorney was present. Flanked by Rangers Arthur and Taliaferro and followed by the attorneys for the defense Morris Norman entered the courtroom. From the night of his arrest and throughout the pretrial contact with him law officers had stated that he had maintained a "smug and cold-blooded attitude." Presumably this meant that he had displayed no emotion. Even when Norman was reported to have tried to apologize to one of the victims during the early investigation of the crime the Texas Ranger that described this to reporters failed to comment on any display of emotion connected with this act. But on this day of his trial he seemed afraid when he entered the crowded courtroom and took his place at the defense table.

Judge Moss called Cause No. 1972 for trial. He propounded to the entire jury panel the principles applicable to the case, the indictment returned by the grand jury, the presumption that the defendant was of sound mind and capable of understanding the nature of his crime, the matter of innocence of the defendant until proven guilty and that the burden of proof rested with the State who would ask that they impose a death sentence upon a guilty verdict. He further instructed the jury panel as to their duty to render judgment only on matters they deemed beyond a reasonable doubt and he ordered that each man be individually qualified on the matter of conscience in assessing the death penalty. Voir dire began by 10:02 a.m. and a jury was selected from the first 20 men of the venire examined. Area newspaper reporters transcribed the story onto their notepads.

The State called only two witnesses, the 45-year-old victim of the brutal attack, Cora Ferris, and County Judge, R. Y. King, who took a confession from the Negro. The confession was admitted in evidence uncontested. Law enforcement lookouts at the north windows behind the spectators could see a crowd of 100 or more men gathering on the court house lawn.

"The victim of the attack took the stand Tuesday morning as the state's main witness. In the oppressive stillness of the crowded courtroom, she haltingly told of the terrors of the dark thicket that Sunday night. Gently prompted by the trial judge, she continued brokenly, revealing the abuses she suffered in the trash littered dump ground. Women spectators, sprinkled throughout the crowd, wept audibly at conclusion of the testimony while grim faced men sat tensely on the edge of their seats."

Perhaps the most convincing evidence in the case was unspoken and needed no introduction into evidence - the sight of 67-year-old Mrs. T. Jones and Miss Ferris. These were ladies well known to the jury and audience to be respectable, credible and naively innocent. Mrs. Jones face was still black and swollen. Miss Ferris was still barely able to walk. The torture of giving her testimony was a sacrificial duty to the cause for justice under the law. During the trial there was not one objection and only one delay. The state rested its case at 11:15 a.m. and the defense was given 15 minutes to prepare its case. At the conclusion of this recess attorney for the defense, Porter, announced that the defense called no witnesses and rested its case.

Arguments started at 1:00 p.m., one and one half hour after state and defense had rested. This phase spanned more time than any other, presumably because it was spent in the Judge's chambers preparing his charge to the jury and with the District Attorney in preparing his argument to the jury. In order to fulfill the statutory requirements for the death penalty there were specific requirements to meet. There would be four counts for them to consider – "criminal attack (the only one carrying the death penalty), assault with intent to attack criminally, and assault and aggravated assault." Historically, laws treated the threat of physical injury as "assault", and the completed act of physical contact as "attack" or battery. "Aggravated assault" was defined as a more serious intent to harm such as through the use of a deadly weapon. [3]

District Attorney Deaver's argument explained these points for the understanding of the jury. In his slow and deliberate manner of making his points [4] he explained the law and gave examples from the testimony. No doubt he quoted from the confession as he would later in his letter to the Texas Prison System's Bureau of Classification. "He said a car light showed him it was two white women and he decided he would attack them." [5] He held the jurymen's eyes to the intensity of purpose they saw in his face as he quoted the words of the victim describing the attack. In a brief moment of silence his eyes moved toward Mrs. Jones and her sister. He assured the jury that based on the evidence presented it would find the defendant guilty of criminal attack. He completed his argument and the jury retired at 1:40 p.m.

"We, as a society of thinking and feeling human beings, struggle within ourselves, ..." Lewis. Nolie Simmons, member of the jury. Photo by Ernest L. Hunt.

At 2:22 p.m. jury returned into open court and jury foreman, C. L. Goin read the verdict:

"We, the jury, find the defendant, Morris Norman, guilty of rape as charged in the indictment and we assess his punishment as death." [6]

Downstairs on the first floor of the Court House voters were casting their votes to elect W. Lee O'Daniel Governor of Texas. Daniels strongly opposed the death penalty, declaring that it should be abolished. [7]

The *Amarillo Daily News* stated that Norman displayed nervousness when the verdict was read. Though he failed to identify his sources that reporter quoted the defendant as stating at the beginning of the trial that he hoped to get two years and that after hearing the testimony he stated that he hoped to have the privilege of serving a life sentence. The court judged him guilty as found by the jury and he retired with his attorneys to decide if he would accept the verdict or appeal it. [8]

"The court-appointed defense attorneys explained to him that he had the privilege of appealing the case. At first he said he wanted to appeal. But when he learned he would have to stay in a Panhandle jail three to six months for the action of the court of criminal appeals he decided he preferred to accept the death sentence. He waived the rights to a two-day period in which he could appeal, and Judge Moss passed sentence." [9]

What motivated his defense attorneys to encourage him to waive appeal is open to debate. Current law would pre-empt any waiver of a death sentence with an automatic appeal, but in the reality of the unfortunate circumstances of that time it was only an option. It was a time when public sentiment for death to a rapist was so pervasive that the possibility of preventing mob violence to enforce it was virtually *nil*. And as long as he was present in a local jail he posed a threat to the safety of that community. The room where the defendant met with his attorneys had a view of the Donley County jail, the snipers stationed in its second floor and the north courthouse lawn where a crowd of men were assembled and waiting. [10]

Aside from the rape issue, the legal perspective on the appeal held by members of the bar of that time was an ethical issue. In a trial in which all parties, prosecution, defense and judge, responsibly carried out their duties to uphold the law under the Constitution there was no reason for an appeal. Failure to prevent cause for appeal was inadequacy of counsel. ". . . they did their duty in their own way, letting themselves out with all the powers they possessed in behalf of their clients and perhaps with their zeal and ability the cases were thoroughly tried, so that appeals were seldom necessary or advisable." [11] Some deliberate maneuvers to create cause for appeal would have been considered by the proponents for a strong Constitutionally driven legal ethic as "employing the use of its form to violate its spirit." [12] Judge Moss, as a member of the State Bar Ethics Committee, was intent on conducting this trial according to the Criminal Procedures of the day. Historically, it was a source of pride for the local bar that they had carried out the trial with record economy of time.[13] Under such pressure of time and the circumstances these principles were admirably executed by the bench, the prosecution and members of the jury. The role of the defense bears the brunt of historical perspective. Against the legal standards of decency of the present age it was inadequate. Against the moral principles of that day and the immediate dangers for the defendant and the citizenry, they responded to a call to duty with no less courage than the soldier who honors his duty to go to war and act under the pressures of battle.

Ethically more questionable were the allegations Norman later made in conversations with prison officials at Huntsville. First, he stated that after his arrest he was kept in a car with the Texas Rangers and threatened until he agreed to sign a confession. [14] Allegation of coerced confessions on the part of Texas Rangers was a sensitive issue when Governor Allred took office. [15]

But by the time of Buddy's arrest Allred had included the matter of the confession in his reform of the Rangers by creating the Ranger Division of Criminal Investigation and training investigators in the more modern methods of interrogation. It is more likely that Rangers Arthur and Taliaferro used these tactics, more manipulative than coercive, to gain his confession. Without overt coercion they could have gained his confession by capitalizing upon his vulnerability to suggestion and appealing to his childlike longing for his mother with implied bargains. [16]

Morris Norman was formally sentenced by Judge Moss at 3:00 p.m. and his execution date was set for Friday, the 16th day of December, A. D., 1938. For his safety Norman was immediately hurried out of the courtroom to a waiting car where he would be transported by Rangers Arthur and Taliaferro to the jail in nearby Memphis. Meanwhile the sheriff waited in Clarendon for the court clerk to prepare the death warrant and commitment papers needed before he could transport the prisoner to the Huntsville State Prison where state executions were carried out. [17]

During the time he was in the Memphis jail for the first time Norman made a public statement during a press conference with a reporter for the Memphis Democrat. This news release was flavored with sensationalism and took some rhetorical liberties with Norman's statement to that reporter. The article stated that Norman deplored his plight stating that before the attack a stranger at the café in colored town had given him a cigarette containing crushed aspirin and hair which caused him to lose his sensibilities. Under such circumstances he committed the crime for which the state would take his life by execution. According to the Rangers standing by in the Memphis jail cell this was a direct contradiction to a previous statement made before the court. As written in the Memphis paper this statement was misleading since Norman made no statement in his trial except that represented in a written confession bearing his signature verified only by the testimony of County Judge, R. Y. King who took the confession.[18] The comment made by the Ranger in the Memphis jail had referred to Norman's statement in that confession. To the Classification Officer in Huntsville Norman later made the allegation that he had been denied the opportunity to testify in his trial.[19]

The issue of his alleged drug intoxication during the commission of the crime had much less legal significance than the public attention it created. Intoxication was no defense. Had there been an argument in his trial from the defense it might have been used to argue against the charge of criminal attack in favor of a charge of assault – the difference between a sentence of death and prison time. More likely it would have served to condemn him more in the eyes of a Saint's Roost jury.

The sensationalism created by the "aspirin cigarette" caused more of a ripple in the press over the state. There was some intrigue involved with the idea that there were some mystical powers in aspirin when mixed with hair and a cigarette but "the aspirin cigarette" served more to peak interest in the trial of Morris Norman. The allegation of a coerced confession to enact "swift justice" was insinuated downstate where public opinion remained biased against the Texas Rangers because of rumors about past use of the "forced confession." In his letter to the Classification Officer, Rev. Earnest Wallace of Bremond, Texas wrote, "I believe that he was just a suspicious character and was scared into saying that he was guilty." [20] There were many factors to challenge in this confession but it seemed to be more plausible than the "aspirin cigarette" story. In any case Morris Norman had made his attempt at a defense while waiting in the Memphis jail. As soon as Sheriff Pierce arrived from Clarendon with the commitment papers he and the Rangers transported their prisoner to Ft. Worth for another night in a safe jail.

It had been a speedy trial, completed and entered into the court minutes and filed away nine days after the commission of the crime. Nine days in which Clarendon was spotlighted upon the stage of all time under examination as a fourth dimension of a time in history in which change was moving faster than the speed of light.

In Austin Jimmy Allred was preparing to leave the Governor's Mansion having accomplished his mission of creating a state police force, the Department of Public Safety. Homer Garrison was entering the second month of the sixty years he would serve as its director with a meritorious test case to the credit of his vision for the department.

In Eastern Germany entire Jewish communities were being destroyed and their inhabitants interned in concentration camps. In London Anthony Eden resigned as England's foreign secretary in protest against Prime Minister Chamberlain's pursuit of the Munich Pact despite Hitler's advancing anti-semantic campaign. In a lecture in Cincinnati Mrs. Franklin D. Roosevelt pleaded for racial tolerance. In Washington proponents for an unregulated radio media were in a heated debate with the Communication Commission in the aftermath of Orson Welles' "War of the World's" broadcast. [21] Aboard H. G. Well's fantasy time machine Orson Welles had crashed into the living rooms of America uninvited and unbridled carrying with him H. G. Wells enduring question:

"What if cruelty had grown into a common passion? What if in this interval the race had lost its manliness, and had developed into something inhuman, unsympathetic, and overwhelmingly powerful?" [22]

In Clarendon, Texas, people waited until Thursday to read their papers. The November 10, 1938 edition of the *Donley County Leader* surveyed their world. The story at the top left was a summary of the nine day saga of the brutal attack and the swift and orderly process of the legal system as it enacted justice. The story commended the way that the southern code of honor in behalf of womanhood had been upheld while feared mob actions had been averted. Across the page was a tribute to Veterans in celebration of Armistice Day. It cried out for world peace and offered a salute from The Editor:

"To the members of the local Post of the American Legion, we congratulate you upon that fine spirit of patriotic community service that has characterized your actions in so many ways here in Clarendon." [23]

American Legionnaires Post 126 assembled in front of the Pastime theatre salute the flag, circa 1943. Photo By Ernest L. Hunt.

Still further across the page was an article paying tribute to the twelve men who served on the jury in the Norman case:

"No mob action was taken because the public had an abiding faith in the kind of men who would sit on the jury. That faith has been further strengthened. Donley County's reputation continues to be that of a place of high grade law-abiding citizenship." [24] As though to speak for the jury, the article paid tribute to the memory of T. Jones, deceased husband of victim Mattie Jones, as "a staunch supporter of the sanctity of the home and protection of womanhood during his entire life." [25]

At the right top of the page was an article whose headlines shared an equal font with the trial story. It welcomed Clarendon College "exes" as they came to a homecoming celebrating the fortieth anniversary of the 1898 founding of the college that had given Clarendon the name of "Athens of the Plains." [26]

In the November 10th issue of *The Clarendon News* there was a tribute from another group of Clarendon citizens. Offering it in the spirit of "the lone white flower tribute" of Bones Hooks, it paid honor to Sheriff Guy Pierce:

"COLORED FOLKS OF CLARENDON THANK SHERIFF

The colored folks of Clarendon wish to commend Sheriff Guy Pierce for the prompt and efficient manner in which he handled the recent disturbance occurring in our section of town.

We regret that one of our race was criminally connected with the offense.

We wish to express our appreciation for the very safe and sane advice given us by Sheriff Pierce during the trouble and for the considerate and constant assurance that no harm would come to those of us who respected law and order.

Bennie Nevile, H. D, McCampbell, Dan Sauls, Manuel Walker: Colored Committee of Clarendon." [27]

In the spotlight for nine days Clarendon wrestled with a volatile matter of societal conscience. It was a time in which across the South men held to a virtually unimpeachable code of honor that decreed the penalty for rape was death. More often this death was being dealt in the form of lynching - tortures, mutilations and property destruction that reached barbaric levels. In 1930 the Sherman and Honey Grove lynchings ignited the sensibilities of Texans. One of these was a woman from Georgetown, Texas, Jessie Daniel Ames. That year she formed the Association of Southern Women for the Prevention of Lynching and drafted a demanding pledge for the association. Through her work in the Methodist Church and among law enforcement officials across the state she gathered signatures to the pledge, which read:

"We declare lynching is an indefensible crime, destructive of all principles of government, hateful and hostile to every ideal of religion and humanity, debasing and degrading to every person involved. ... Public opinion has accepted too easily the claim of lynchers and mobsters that they are acting solely in defense of womanhood. In light of the facts we dare no longer to permit this claim to pass unchallenged, nor allow those bent on personal revenge and savagery to commit acts of violence and lawlessness in the name of women. We solemnly pledge ourselves to create a new public opinion in the South, which will not condone for any reason whatever, acts of mobs or lynchings. We will teach our children at home, at school and at church a new interpretation of law and religion. We will assist all officials to uphold their oath of office, and finally, we will join with every minister, editor, school teacher and patriotic citizen in a program of education to eradicate lynchings and mobs forever from our land." [28]

It remains unknown if there were any Clarendon signatures on this pledge but there can be no doubt that the spirit of it was present among the citizenry that came together so quickly and acted with such singleness of purpose and principle. Even though they had sentenced a young man to die for his crime they had treated him with respect and had enacted their concept of justice within the law of their time. It exemplified what fifty years later Chief Justice Warren would call "the progress of a maturing society." [29]

The dust devil that had swirled into their midst and caught up the lives of its citizens and thrashed them in its frenzy left Clarendon. Men had stepped forward and performed their duties with valor and single-ness of purpose. But in stepping back from the scene they descended into a deep silence about the cause for which they had acted. The whole community adopted a persona of nobility toward the unspeakable crime. For 75 years the actions of these men would be remembered only for having done it swiftly and in behalf of law and order. The wounded women, their lives changed forever, would remain hidden beneath the debris, forgotten for the persons they were and even for the valor with which they confronted the storm.

Down the time continuum, the spider trail left by this whirlwind remained and the dust devil moved toward another community. There it would hold a citizenry for another nine days in its limelight as that community spoke out for a different facet of justice.

9

The Rover – Goin' Home

Norman's meeting with his mother was a promise made to him as a part of an informal plea bargain. His fear of never seeing his mother again was as strong a motivator for waiving his right to appeal the death sentence as his fear of a lynching. The Rangers had first spotted his longing for his mother as they began their interrogation with general questions about family. As his defense attorneys explained the dangers inherent in waiting out the appeal process in a local jail, they mentioned the possibility of never seeing his mother again. Though it is only assumed that he was offered the promise of a last visit with her as encouragement for signing the waiver, it is a credit to the integrity of the Rangers and the sheriff who had first taken his confession that they honored this last wish.

Lizzie Norman lived in the remote Beck Prairie community in northern Robertson County. Her husband, Wesley, was a tenant farmer and she did laundry and housework for white families there. This couple had been a part of Robertson County since the late 1880's when Wesley Norman arrived with his parents and some of his younger siblings from Upper Fishing Creek, North Carolina and Lizzie's family had migrated westward from East Texas to the Brazos River Valley. In their

youth Wesley and Lizzie had lived with their families as neighbors in
the plantation style cotton farming industry. Later, during their marriage, they had transformed along with the people of that area through
the Reconstruction Era to the breakup of the plantations and into the
smaller tenant farmer system.[1]

The Beck Prairie people had carried forward the plantation commu-
nal style between landlord and tenant. They looked out for each other
and for the families that worked for them. Typically, the tenant families
lived in a shanty located somewhere on the property of the landlord and
though their status was subservient, they were treated as family. Often,
in some communities, the black people attended church services with
the white citizens. There, race created no barriers between neighbors in
times of need.[2] It was at such a time for Lizzie that her primary contact
with the outside world, her rural mail carrier, R.H. Stellbauer, of nearby
Bremond, reached out to her.[3] At her mailbox he always had time to
visit with her and if there was a letter for her, he read it to her because
she had never learned to read.

When the local newspapers first printed the news of Morris Norman's
crime, Mr. Stellbauer became concerned. He knew that Lizzie had
known little of the whereabouts or activities of her son after he left home
almost two years before, and he realized that she knew nothing now of
his situation. He made the decision to break this news to her. Standing
beside her rural mailbox he unfolded his personal copy of a newspaper
and read it to her. He also made known his indignation that the representatives of the legal system had not advised her about the crime or the
upcoming trial. In his statement to the law enforcement officers, Morris
had said that he was not sure that his parents were still living where
he had left them because his letters to them had gone unanswered.[4]
In Donley County this was enough to justify not notifying Norman's
mother of his arrest. Lawmen there feared her presence might ignite
the mob violence that was boiling just beneath the surface, putting both
his family and her son in danger.

On their way from the Ft. Worth jail to Death Row in Huntsville on November 9th the lawmen took Norman to his mother's home in Beck Prairie to meet with Lizzy, Wesley and brother, Walter. [5]   For security reasons, Sheriff Pierce and Rangers Arthur and Taliaferro carefully guarded their prisoner and cut short the time available for outsiders to the visit to gather.   One of the Rangers reported that Buddy admitted his guilt to an older lady at the scene but told his mother that he had not committed the crime, a thing he knew she wanted to believe.[6] No doubt she prayed for him in the melodic mother's tones with which she had surrounded him since he was the sickly baby she carried on a pillow.   Apart from his mother as he was leaving the older woman admonished him,

"Boy, you better pray." [7]

She directed the prayer, in song,

"I am troubled, I am troubled.
I'm troubled in mind.
If Jesus don't help me
I surely will die. [8]
"Jesus, remember me." [9]

With this Lizzie and Morris parted forever.

As the patrol car carrying her son turned onto the county road from the single rut trail to her tenant shack, Lizzie's mind drifted backward.

She lifted his listless body from the pillow cradled on her lap and pled with him to take her engorged nipple.   His reflexive attempt to suckle evoked a shrill gasp from his throat and he vomited the milk that had trickled there into her hands.   In a private setting where she could allow her tears she held the frail form to her breast and with her body swaying and eyes half-closed, she sang, lifting to heaven her anguish with the slave songs long familiar to her race.[10]

"There is Balm in Gilead,
To make the wounded whole. . .
Come here, Jesus, come here, please." [11]

His struggle sustained for then, he slept and she returned him to the vomit stained pillow to await the cruelty reserved for him at a later time.

Later the morning of November 9, 1938, Morris Norman was admitted to the Texas Prison System at Huntsville. Even though he had waived his right to an appeal within the trial system, his right to an appeal for clemency was honored within his initial death row processing. As a part of Governor Allred's legal reform of the state police force and criminal procedures, he had also streamlined the commutation process. Members of the newly formed Board of Pardons and Parole ("BPP") were instructed to obtain a social history, a classification study, of every death row inmate upon admission. Prison officers with the newly formed Bureau of Classification interviewed the condemned men and collected materials such as letters from friends and family that were forwarded at their request, to the BPP in the event an appeal for clemency was initiated in behalf of the prisoner.[12]

In addition, prison officials sent letters to previous employers, schoolteachers and principals, county welfare or relief personnel, and personal friends or contacts that might be able to provide information related to later appeals for clemency. These letters contained questions about the inmate's character (e.g., dependability, use of alcohol, ambition, honesty, intelligence)." [13] On Saturday, November 11, 1938, twenty-four such letters in behalf of Morris Norman were sent out from the Bureau of Classification. [14]

Within days the letters from Robertson county citizens began to paint a very different portrait of the boy who had grown up in their community. They called him Buddy. Prison officers began to explore and assess the workings of a different kind of mind. Criminal history checks and correspondence with relief agencies and CCC officers in Illinois chronicled the transformation of Buddy. What happened beside a dump ground in Donley County on October 30, 1938 challenges the latest scientific understandings of today about how the nurturing of the brain of a child become the actions of the man. [15]

In the initial interviews with the classification officers, Buddy stayed with his story about the "asparine cigarette." His fanciful elaborations upon that version of the attacks confirmed its lack of credibility. The very fact that he recalled specific details about the crime scene and the chronology of what happened cast doubt on his allegations of having lost his sensibilities due to the effects of the cigarette. Though he claimed he wrote letters home and he made statements to the investigating officers in Donley County that he understood the contents of the confession he was signing, prison interviewers as well as the people in his home community declared him illiterate. He had a keen memory for some things but his way of reasoning about them was baffling. The version of the attack he gave prison officials was:

"After returning to town and was starting to roll a Bull Durham cigarette a Negro stranger, tall, slender, and slightly older than the subject, offered him a cigarette from a Camel package. He accepted this cigarette and after smoking it almost immediately a sudden dizziness seized him. He began staggering up the street out of town, falling down several times. After proceeding about two or three hundred yards, his staggerings and fallings down brought him up facing in the opposite direction on the opposite side of the street. While proceeding out of town he noticed two women on the far side of the street going in the same direction as he, and after his position was reversed he suddenly saw these women in front of him, but too late to veer to one side. The impact of their running together carried the three of them into the ditch, the subject being in more contact with one woman than the other. He states that he scrambled to his feet and said, '"Why in the hell don't you watch where you are going, or someone is going to get hurt?"' And then he staggered down the street to his room at the café, pulled off his clothes and went to sleep." [16]

For those familiar with the Clarendon streets involved in the scene as described, there is an obvious confusion of directions and distances. This account was dismissed by prison officials as rationalization of his guilt and of his intelligence it was stated: "His vocabulary and language are limited and his mannerisms are those of the average tenant farm negro."[17] This was a typical stereotyping found in the files of Negro death row inmates.

For Buddy those troubled early years had sealed his destiny. His mother, Lizzie, related those details verbally to the Robertson County Caseworker, Mrs. A. W. Klawelter, as her response to the social history form sent to her by the prison Bureau of Classification on November 11th. When he was 1 month old he was in size "equal to a 5 month old child." But then he had the whooping cough and after he recovered from that he was so frail that he had to be carried on a pillow. At age two he injured his head in a fall from a swing. He still carries that scar on his forehead. He was slow to learn. Wesley contributed comments about Buddy's 1936 arrest for disorderly drinking in Bremond, stating that after a few days he was turned loose. In the presence of her husband Lizzie told the social worker that while Buddy did not have interests or ambition he was willing to do whatever he was told to do. She stated that he was easy to control and did not receive severe punishment at home.[18]

The letters from neighbors and employers of the Normans responding to the Bureau of Classification's requests for letters of references revealed a very different version of Buddy's treatment by his father. Mr. Stellbauer, the mail carrier, stated that the last year Buddy lived in Robertson he stayed with the family of a black farmer named Mose Dean and his wife in order to escape the terrible beatings of his father. "I might add," continued Mr. Stellbauer, "his father's reputation in this community is not very good; . . . he is mean and overbearing." [19]

Miss Lorene Stephenson, a young schoolteacher living in the community, stated that Buddy "roved about a lot" because he could not get along with his father. Both Matt Davis, Assistant Cashier of the Calvert State Bank and owner of a dry goods store in that town, and T.J. Smith, President of the bank, spoke about Buddy's roving. Mr. Davis excused it with a comment from Buddy's father that the boy never had good sense. The Classification Summary characterized Buddy as "an unstable individual who has been unable to adjust adequately to his home environment." [20]

There was community awareness of Buddy's abuse by his father but this was a time in which public opinion and even the courts held that unless parental abuse exceeded the bounds of reason and humanity, parents had the right to raise their children as they saw fit. There was no such thing as child protective services. If there was help it came from family and neighbors willing to get involved. [21] Mose Dean was such a neighbor. He opened his home to Buddy. Lorene Stephenson whose family's farm adjoined the Dean place, made him welcome to come into hers and play with the abundant supply of toys that belonged to her brother. Her older brother, Ernest, enjoyed watching Buddy and his little brother "feel rich" when he gave them a dime. Mr. Stellbauer always checked to see that he was standing in the lane beside the rural mailbox as he daily delivered the Dean mail. Both banker Smith and merchant Davis took the time to give him a ride home when they encountered him roving the roadways in the area. [22]

It is unknown if Lizzie was also a victim of her husband's overbearing nature but the overwhelming respect and support from the community that encircled her was quick to come forth. In all of the letters of reference she was characterized as humble, hardworking and very religious. Six days after Buddy's trial in Clarendon twenty-four prominent citizens from all parts of Robertson County signed a formal appeal to the Board of Pardons and Appeals asking for clemency. The appeal was based on his reputation for abiding by the law, his parents reputation as poor and humble law abiding citizens and upon his condition as uneducated and "weak minded." [23]

Ironically, Buddy was on death row for committing rape and unspeakable indignities upon the person of a humble, hardworking farm lady known for her impeccable reputation as a moral and religious woman. In defending the honor of this lady 12 men, all but one a farmer, had sentenced him to death for his crime. Out of respect for his mother, an equally hardworking farm lady with an undisputed reputation as a moral and religious lady, 24 men, all but two farmers, were appealing for his clemency. Except for the difference of race the two ladies were equals, virtually the same age and position of regard in their respective communities. [24]

Citizens of Clarendon were indignant when word of the appeal reached them. An article in the *Donley County Leader* vowed that influential citizens across the Panhandle would launch a vigorous protest to the Board of Pardons and Parole to uphold the death sentence for what was termed "the most heinous crime in the annals of Panhandle criminal history."[25] Of course the term "influential citizens" insinuated those with political clout, for the BPP was in fact made up of political appointees. While Governor Allred's reform of the board had been made in an effort to reduce the governor's role in the clemency process and therefore the possibility of political corruption, "influence" with the board was still a reality. [26]

There were other factors in the makeup and function of the BPP that would play more deciding roles in the final outcome of Buddy's case. The newly formed board consisted of three members: one appointed by the governor, another by the chief justice of the Texas Supreme Court and another by the presiding Judge of the Texas Court of Criminal Appeals. These men maintained separate offices and communicated by telephone or letter only and did not hold formal board meetings. Board members were not accountable to legal statutes, public or legislative bodies or to judicial oversight. Board decisions were recommendations only to the governor.[27] Three quarters of a century down the time continuum that decision of the BPP represents a revealing window on the inner workings of the moral conscience of that time - no clemency for those convicted of rape, especially for those of color. In the evolution of Supreme Court decisions since, rape is no longer a capital offense, but controversy over the question of death eligibility and intellectual disability only becomes more heated.

Citizens of Donley County were shocked to think anyone would consider clemency for such a heinous crime. Citizens of Robertson County could not comprehend that their Buddy was capable of such a thing. Mose Dean wrote: "I have a house full of young girls while he lived with me with no trouble. He never seemed to care for girl company some how." Dean went on to name three white families in the neighborhood that felt safe in leaving their wives and children alone with Buddy. [28]

Letters of reference from Rev. Earnest Wallace, farmer and part time pastor, and Paul W, Rehberg, hotel owner, spoke of their experiences of entrusting their wives and daughters to the presence of Buddy. Miss Lorene Stephenson was a young woman in her late teens when she allowed him in her home for hours at a time. [29]

Her appeal in behalf of his mental incapacities was poignant and insightful beyond her time. "His feeble mind must have caused him to get into that trouble. He did wrong and needs to be punished, but does he deserve death?" [30] Even after the 2002 Supreme Court decision in the *Virginia v. Atkins* case that states that we do not execute the mentally incapacitated, we continue to be stymied by how to define that state. No doubt, we continue to execute brain injured and mentally defected individuals as long as we continue to execute.

If the people of Donley County noted his mental condition certainly no mention of it was made. In fact it was conspicuously missing in the area press coverage while it was consistently mentioned in coverage in other areas of the state and nation. The local citizenry saw only his act and the pressing need to maintain order. Their compassion was focused upon the victims. The people of Robertson County remembered Buddy as a weak-minded boy with little or no understanding of how or why he was that way. Mr. Stellbauer wrote: "Morris did not act like an average Negro boy, but why I do not know. I never saw him smile in my life." Others noted his perpetual wanderings always in the name of seeking work. Mr. Henry J. Perry called him "sorry" because of the impetuous characteristics that gave him the nickname among his Negro peers of "Must Have It." [31] Whatever was to become of him as a man did not factor. He left them remembering only the boy standing motionless beside the road with no expression on his face seemingly not knowing where he had been, only longing to come home. Almost unnoticed he wandered away from them into manhood in quite a different world.

10

From Chicago to Clarendon

W HEN HE FIRST made contact with the Travelers Aid Society at the
historic LaSalle Street Railway Station in Chicago late on the
night of November 28, 1937 he claimed to have only recently arrived in
the Chicago area for the first time aboard a private plane. The story he
told the Travelers Aid worker was that he had a job with a barnstorming
pilot to clean out his plane as he traveled about the country. But that
week when they landed at a small airport outside of Chicago the pilot
suddenly dismissed him without paying him for his work. [1] Buddy later
told the same story to the officers at the Texas Prison system but he
gave the date of his arrival as May of 1937. In the family history given
the Texas Prison system his mother stated that he left home for the last
time on this same date. [2] The discrepancies in these dates can easily be
explained by the circumstances surrounding Buddy's contact with the
Travelers Aid.

The Travelers Aid Society was a welfare agency originally founded
to give assistance to immigrants who arrived in America at sea ports. As
the general migration patterns sent many people traveling westward, the
work of the agency was expanded to offer aid to weary and bewildered
travelers who were stranded in the railways and wagon yards along the
way. The agency continued to expand into the crowded urban areas

during the Great Depression. Aid workers were stationed in railroad terminals to assist newly arrived travelers who were stranded to find suitable lodging, appropriate social services and employment. During this time an added mission was to return run-away children and youths to their relatives. [3] This was Buddy's appeal to them.

For an undetermined time he had been homeless and "walking the streets of Chicago." He claimed to have been arrested earlier that month on a drunkenness charge and later for vagrancy.[4] Wandering about the downtown railway yards he was cold and hungry and he wanted to go home. He had appealed to a policeman in the vicinity for assistance in returning to Texas and was directed to the LaSalle Street Station, or he was taken there in lieu of another arrest by a policeman who spotted him trying to hop a train bound for home. At the station he was interviewed by an Aid worker. It was a sensitive worker who chronicled the visit with Buddy with revealing details about the human he was and the path he had traveled from the Brazos River Valley of Texas to the jungle of Chicago's Southside.

"Mr. Norman was a dark skinned colored man with prominent Negroid features and a noticeable scar running lengthwise on his forehead. He spoke in a slow, stuttering fashion and the information which he gave about his situation was rather vague.

Mr. Norman stated that his parents, Lizzie and Wesley, work on a farm in Bremond, Texas, and have been known to the relief agency in that community although he did not believe that they were on relief when he left home three weeks before. He stated that he was the oldest of seven children there and he left home to secure employment in order to assist his family. He stated that he had quit school when he was in the second grade five years before. He had been away from home before on several occasions but never so far away from home. He had never previously asked for assistance to return, always having hitchhiked back." [5]

Not only was the Travelers Aid worker sensitive to the human needs she saw in Buddy but she was obviously a well-trained representative of an emerging school of psychiatry called humanism. This approach emphasized the personal worth of an individual and the human capacity to overcome hardship, pain and despair. The goal of agencies such as Travelers Aid was to provide opportunities for individuals to exercise this capacity. [6]

That night he was given a place to sleep off of the streets at one of the Newberry Shelters and advised to contact the Transportation Service of the Chicago Relief Administration the next day. [7] There he described his family and his work history in the Bremond area of Robertson County. He stated that his primary work there had been in farm labor but that he had worked in a garage in Bremond for eighteen months. In this interview he did not mention his job with the barnstorming pilot but stated that he had left his garage job in Bremond to join the Eastern Star Rodeo. [8] There were a number of inconsistencies and jumbled dates in the history that Buddy gave the Chicago relief agencies. Obviously, he was trying to tell a story that would qualify him for relief aid. Without this as a motivator he told much of the same story to classification officers at the Texas Prison system and to the law officers that took his statement in Clarendon. The prison officials were able to clarify dates and corroborate the majority of his account of his life after May of 1937. [9]

His mention of the Eastern Star Rodeo to the Chicago Relief Administration was not found elsewhere, but it was plausible. For young men around the Ft. Worth area where performances of this rodeo were a part of the fall Ft. Worth Livestock Show, it represented the glamour of being a rodeo star. Boasting of such things seemed to be common with Buddy, perhaps because he needed fantasy to add excitement to his lackluster life. As it turned out this was a significant clue to his psychopathology. For then it was just another boast not supported by logic. To be a star in the Eastern Star Rodeo required advanced rodeo skills that took time and work to achieve. Buddy's history did not include hard work and the verified timeline of his life did not include a time for this adventure. [10]

He more often told the tale of how he had encountered a barnstorming pilot in Mart, Texas, and went to work for him "cleaning out the plane." He reported that in this capacity he had made several trips to Illinois, the last one being sometime in May when he was kicked off the plane without his wages and left to find his way into Chicago. In actual fact there was a young man from Mart who after receiving flight training in Maryland in 1937 had returned to his home town to provide the "one dollar joy rides" to the public that were so popular during the last of the barnstorming days. One flaw in Buddy's story about the pilot he worked for was that he stated that he was from Los Angeles, California, not a native of Mart. Buddy may have wanted to add glamour to the qualifications of his boss or just may have fabricated the whole story. [11]

Buddy could have simply "hitchhiked" into Chicago. His wanderings as a child had taught him how to do that. On July 29, 1937, he was arrested in Crown Point, Indiana, on charges of "train riding" as he was possibly on his way to Chicago. In his statement to the classification officers he talked knowledgably about the geography within a 200 mile radius around Chicago. [12]

He claimed to have worked as a porter and night watchman during the months of May and June, 1937, for the Alvin Crosley Garage at 4749 East 47th Street in Chicago. Inquiries about this employment were returned to the Bureau of Classification unclaimed. What was really occurring in the life of Buddy during the summer of 1937 is largely unknown. After the Indiana arrest the first verified accounting was in August when he was identified as a resident at 4600 Calumet during the fall months of 1937. This was the boarding house he claimed was a house of ill repute where Buddy claimed to have procured clients for black and white prostitutes. A transformed Buddy came to light. He had been absorbed by the seamier side of Chicago. His fantasies of grandeur shifted. The boasts he made in Clarendon about procuring for this house were likely accurate though not exactly in the way he boasted. [13]

Procuring, the legal term, and pimping, the more common street word, in Chicago, as in all larger cities, was a big gang driven business with a hierarchy of gang lords involved. Being a pimp equated to having money, power and respect. A graphic account of the world of a pimp in Chicago in 1938 was told by Iceberg Slim in his autobiography, *Pimp*. Slim was reputed to be "the best known pimp of our time." He was representative of young blacks who were leaving the south in an effort to break free of the servitude forced on them in that culture. He was conceived in a small town in Tennessee but born in the "promised land up North in Chicago" the same year that Buddy was born in Texas. Interestingly, Slim left the red light district of Rockford, Illinois, where he grew up to return to Chicago just as Buddy left Chicago for Camp Durand near Rockford. Slim painted a vivid picture of his fantasies of a grander life in the role of a pimp. Perhaps the words of Iceberg Slim echoed the dreams in Buddy's mind:

"I felt powerful and beautiful. I would see myself gigantic and powerful like God Almighty. My clothes would glow. My suits were spun-gold shot through with precious stones. My shoes would be dazzling silver. Everybody in both worlds would kiss your ass if you had flash and front."

These were the dreams. The realities of that world represented man at his cruelest. It was a drug infested world of brute violence, of bribes, of betrayals and retaliation. It was a perverse world where oral copulation was commonly practiced and even more commonly spoken of. It was a world of cruelty where brutality was a mandate for rule breakers. It was a "hate club" from which there was no escape. With the status of an Iceberg Slim, a pimp was in charge of advertising his girls, maintaining control of a turf for their operation and sheltering them from the legal consequences of their activities. This required cunning, vigilance, political clout and hard work. That Buddy had ever attained that level of prowess in the street world of Chicago is doubtful, but he had too much understanding of its ways not to have been some part of it.

Within the hierarchy, an established house of prostitution had room for a "chili pimp" of lesser prowess, a pimp with one girl only or a hustler who advertised the services out on the streets. The madam or residential pimp of such a house worked under a lord pimp who guarded the "turf" and provided political clout with law enforcement. In 1938 South Calumet Street was lined with boarding houses such as the one at 4600 South Calumet. This area was reputed to be a "red light district" in South Chicago. [14]

Morris Norman resided in the rear basement flat of this Chicago boarding house at 4600 Calumet, From August through November, 1937. Illustration by Charles Lyles.

At the request of the Texas Prison's Bureau of Classification an Illinois Parole Agent called at the southwest corner of Calumet and 46th Street to verify Buddy's claim that he had procured for the residents of this boarding house. Agent Fisher interviewed a lady who lived next door and acted as the landlady and rent collector for the house. From the Classification mug shot she positively identified him as the young man who resided in the basement flat in the rear of the large rambling structure during the months of August, September, October and November of 1937. She stated that he was an errand boy for the various kitchenette managers in the neighborhood, including herself, and that his services were given in an upright manner. Several roomers of the 4600 Calumet residence were also interviewed. None of them were willing to make a positive identification but did verify that Buddy's Texas Prison System mug shot did resemble a young man that used to live in the basement flat.[15] Penalties for giving information about their operation to the law as spelled out in Slim's history – severe punishments from the pimp hierarchy- gives a reasonable explanation for their reluctance to make any positive statement about Buddy. It served more to verify his claim than to refute it.

On November 21, 1938, the Chicago officer making the call at Buddy's former residence for the Texas Classification Officer referred the case on to "a colored investigator" because he was more qualified to determine the veracity of Buddy's claim about procuring there.[16] Such a maneuver was consistent with Slim's account of how some police officers were bribed. Forestalling would render the matter moot on December 16.

The possibility of the political clout of a true pimp may have been at play. Or even if not, within the pimp business there was an internal structure built around violence that dealt with rule breakers. There were harsh punishments for the prostitutes. One who "crossed" or informed or ran away from her pimp or withheld his fee was obliged to receive a savage beating. The prowess of a pimp depended upon his ability to enforce this savagery. Slim's finesse at meting out this underworld justice with no show of emotion earned him the name of Iceberg. The structure of that system was also such that if the law was brought in the prostitute would bear the brunt of the consequences.[17] Any more information about the true operations at 4600 South Calumet was not found in the Inmate File of Morris Norman. That such a world even existed was beyond the comprehension of the people of Clarendon. There the fantasy of grandeur for the colored man was reflected in Marble Eye. That of the white youth in Clarendon was driving down Main Street in a convertible wearing a gold watch.

During the latter part of 1937 while he lived in the Newberry shelter, Buddy also worked for a used furniture dealer on East 55th Street as a truck driver and helper. The letter of reference from Mr. Gould, the store owner, praised his honesty, dependability and good character. He stated that he routinely trusted Buddy with large sums of money and he credited him as being ambitious, hardworking and intelligent. He reported that he left sometime after the first of the year to further his career with a better job. Gould did not mention the CCC as he possibly did not know that this was Buddy's "better job." Like the people from Robertson County Gould could not believe that Buddy was capable of such a crime. He, too, blamed the possibility of "bad company" for his downfall. He asked that he be kept informed of the outcome of Buddy's case hoping it would be for the best. [18]

Buddy told classification officers at the prison that in November of 1937 he had been arrested for drunkenness and jailed for five days. Near the same time he reported that he had been arrested for vagrancy. The Illinois Parole Agency could not positively verify the arrest and jail time for drunkenness but did verify the matter of the vagrancy. He had been arrested, investigated and released on that charge. Gould evidently did not know about these problems, chose to ignore them or misrepresent them to the Bureau of Classification, for this was the same November that Buddy had wandered into the LaSalle Railway Station. The Chicago Transportation service tried in vain to contact Texas for travel assistance back to Texas. Meanwhile the Relief Administration put him in one of their boarding homes until they helped him joined the CCC in January.[19]

It seems there had been some kind of break with the Calumet connection. Was it just another time that Morris "had failed to give job satisfaction" in the term used by Mr. Stellbauer to describe his behavior patterns, or had something else happened? The Illinois State Parole Agent's report from his call to 4600 Calumet included an incident reported by the long time janitor for the boarding house. The janitor stated that in November of 1937 the property had changed owners and that the rent collector for the building at that time, a man known as "Mc", had disappeared with the rent money. Had the disappearance of "Mc" and a new owner created an eviction for Buddy? Had he broken rank within the pimping hierarchy or quarreled with one of his ladies as he had with the girl in Clarendon? What had prompted the vagrancy charge? Or had November of 1937 just been another time in his cycle of wanderings when he was standing beside a road wanting to go home to his mother? From Chicago there was no road home, just a turn in the road that would carry Buddy to a very different life. [20]

One of the first projects launched by President Franklin Roosevelt after his election in 1933 was the Civilian Conservation Corps, more commonly called The Tree Army. The plan was to put up to 500,000 unemployed youths to work in forests, parks, and rangelands to rescue eroding natural resources. The Army would run the camps; the agriculture and interior departments would be responsible for the work projects. Roosevelt lauded his program for the way it provided and trained the youth for actual work. Idealistically, in one of his radio broadcasts addressed to the young men of the CCC he proclaimed:

"Through you the nation will graduate a fine group of strong young men, clean-living, trained to self-discipline and above all, willing and proud to work for the joy of working."

Many World War I veterans were eventually hired by the program to train and oversee the youth. Prominent citizens in the locale of each camp supported and offered a spirit of mentoring for the young men. [21] If Buddy's father's anger with him had been based on his inability to keep a job and contribute to the support of his family and Buddy's shiftlessness had been the result of a lack of paternal nurturing, this was a made to order plan for him – at least in theory.

The CCC assigned Buddy to Camp Durand in the northern part of Illinois. Here a troop of 100 to 164 Negro recruits carried out a program to battle erosion of the rich farmland in that area. There years of heavy rains had washed away much of the rich top soil and scarred the landscape with deep gullies. Wielding shovels and mattocks these young men would build 30 miles or more of terraces in a work season. They built dams made of brush and timber across the gullies and dug up sod to line drainage channels. Where hillsides had caved off into bare slopes they built sod lined trenches that encircled the slopes to fortify them against the erosion. While most the work was hand labor there were at least two pieces of government owned machinery. With a rock crusher they crushed limestone donated from nearby quarries to be used by the farmers to check certain areas of erosion. A tractor the size of a garden tractor of today was with a special rotary implement that bit into the earth and slung it to either side to form a small trench. [22] Buddy may have operated this machine or at least was trained to. He was classified as a tractor driver. [23]

Work, and hard work, was the daily routine of Camp Durand troops but they also had recreation activities. In the era when Joe Lewis reigned as a black hero, boxing was a favorite. At camp they were given instruction and time to work out. In nearby Rockford, Illinois, the boyhood home of Iceberg Slim, they were invited to use the newly constructed gym for an hour set aside for local colored boxers to work out. Some of the Camp Durand boxers were entered in an area Golden Gloves tournament. [24] There is nothing recorded to indicate that Buddy included boxing in his hero fantasies but the way he carried out the attack on his victims was as though he had entered the ring to face not one but two opponents and that he had to act quickly to save the round. One local newspaper quoted him, presumably from his official confession, as having said, "There were two of them and that was too much." [25] What bell went off in his mind to unleash his attack will forever remain a mystery but in reality life at Camp Durand had toned his body with an incredible strength and in that setting a predominant image of physical prowess was that of the champion prize fighter.

Around the world of that era boxing was a favorite sport. It easily accessed vast audiences through the media of radio and motion pictures. It made big money for promoters, especially in the numbers racket. Boxing became entangled in worldwide cultural, racial and political conflicts in the championship dual between Joe Louis and Max Schmeling. With its fervor for the sport, Rockford was a natural site for promotion of the Louis-Schmeling fight. Louis was cast in the role of a Superman like hero fighting for truth, justice and the American way and Schmeling as the sporting symbol of the tyrannical Nazi regime.

In Rockford on the night of the Louis-Schmeling championship fight the community was ready to celebrate. The Palace Theater advertised its plans to broadcast the event:

"The Palace Theater will stop its show to offer a radio broadcasting of the Louis-Schmeling fight over a special loudspeaker. Motion pictures of the fight will be shown at the Palace starting Saturday night."

A Rockford nightspot advertised"
"At The Cave tonight
Big Jack Dempsey Party.
We Are Introducing Jack Dempsey to Rockford
Free Souvenirs and Free Dancing for All Tonight."

With Buddy's talent for gravitating to the action spots it is not hard to image him being in Rockford that night. [26]

Buddy's hero fantasies were being charged by the social ferment boiling out of the ominous storm forming over the globe. On North Jefferson Street in Clarendon, where he was destined to find his final action spot, a loudspeaker was set up midway down North Jefferson Street courtesy of Kerbow's Furniture Store. Proud of their dealership of the latest in radio sets and naive in their images of an excited and jubilant crowd of colored people rejoicing for the victory of their hero, the Kerbow brothers went all out to stage the broadcast. They enlisted the voluntary services of freelance photographer, Ernest Hunt, to record the celebration with his flash camera. They arranged for chairs and set up an arena to accommodate the crowd.

Albert "Marble Eye" Boyd in the fedora, mingles in the crowd
of spectators to a radio broadcast of the Louis-Schmeling
fight, June 26, 1938. Photo by Ernest L. Hunt.

As it turned out the adults took the chairs and the young black boys dressed in their Depression Era rags sat at the feet of Marble Eye. He was attired in a starched white shirt, dark gabardine slacks and black banded Fedora hat. The fight came on and quickly ended in victory for Joe Lewis, the Brown Bomber. But there was no rejoicing from the crowd, including Marble Eye. They appeared bored or oppressed as though they felt obligated to endure the patronizing gesture of the white people without understanding why. After puzzling over the pictures the Kerbows and their friends came to a sobering realization. Few if any of the citizens of colored town owned a radio. Few of them could read a newspaper. Lewis was no hero to them. They simply did not know who he was. [27]

As it turned out his brief service in the Tree Army gave Buddy the chance to be a hero to his family. The CCC soldiers were paid $30 per month but since they were fed and their needs maintained in camp it was thought it was best not to have the youth with any excess money to spend. They were required to put $25 of their pay into a deposit account. If their family qualified for relief this money could be sent to them. In May of 1938 a letter was dictated from him to his commanding officer stating that even though he thought he had lost contact with his family, his mother had somehow found out that he was in the Tree Army and had sent him a letter telling him that his father's health was bad and he was unable to work and support his family of eight. Buddy signed this typed request for his family to receive an allotment from his deposit fund. [28]

In her letter of reference to the Bureau of Classification the Robertson County schoolteacher, Lorene Stephenson, wrote:

"I don't believe his family knew where he was for a long time or how he got in the CCC." But after they got the first allotment check she continued, "I heard one of the little boys said, 'We are rich now!'" [29]

No doubt this was a kind of victory for Buddy, but his life in the Army did not change him. He was trained as a tractor driver which was something he knew to begin with. His commanding officer stated that with close supervision his work was satisfactory but not even the Army could contain his roving. Apparently he would leave camp for as long as a week at a time. In his letter to the Bureau of Classification, Captain Louis Earlix, Assistant Adjutant General, quoted from Buddy's misconduct record:

"April 9, 1938: Enrollee sold a watch which was not his property to another enrollee. Upon being accused he first stated that he bought the watch and later claimed that he found it and made an effort to locate the rightful owner; August 25, 1938: Confined within Camp limits for a period of one week for failure to clean his barracks properly; August 3, 1938: extra duty for breaking the confinement within Camp limits for one week; September 13, 1938: dishonorable discharged from the CCC as punishment for again breaking confinement and refusal to perform extra duty given for disciplinary purposes."

At the time of his discharge he gave his future address as 561 South St. Paul Avenue, Beloit, Wisconsin just across the state line from Durand, Illinois. [30]

On October 11, 1938 he was arrested in Beloit for vagrancy. [31] Quite often this charge was used by law enforcement as a warning to cease engaging in some other criminal activity or face a more serious charge. A vagrancy charge often served as an invitation to move on. After his release from that charge in Chicago he did not return to the Calumet Street boarding house but showed up in the La Salle train station seeking a way out of Chicago. Immediately after his release on that charge in Beloit he stole rides on trains that took him through Kansas City and into the Texas Panhandle where he found work picking cotton.

Buddy's account to the prison officials about how the liquor was obtained in colored town was much the same as young Clarendon men of that era described it many years later. A request was made by a knock on the door of the home where Buddy was rooming and confirmed with a five dollar bill. If the bootlegger was assured that "the coast was clear," the customer could return later to the door and be handed a pint of whiskey. In the scene that Buddy described about procuring the whiskey for the white boys he acted as the go between the boys and the knock on the door. Research into how a girl was procured remains speculation. The same folkloric history that described bootlegging in that time indicated that girls were acquired in much the same speakeasy style. The girls reputedly lived with their families and after the knock on the door procedure a door would open and the girls would be available.[32] Buddy's claim to have already been procuring for a Clarendon prostitute for the week that he had been in the area did not seem logical. Perhaps this was only more of Buddy's boasting that so quickly he had become a part of the scene. Another intriguing possibility is that as a "chili pimp"[33] he actually brought the girl with him from Beloit and that he envisioned himself as pimp working North Jefferson Street with his own girl.

How the dates were carried out that night also had to be unusual. According to Buddy's account of it the girl and her customers were near or on the side of the very road that the victims had routinely traveled toward home after church every Sunday night for years. Their habitual route was to skirt around the edge of colored town on the east until they past the dump ground. At that point their path took a curve to the west into that corner of colored town and connected with Highway 18 that took them to the lane leading to their country home. Had the church service that night ended a short time earlier the ladies would have walked through the bedroom of Buddy's girlfriend. As it happened they met near the dump grounds at an intersection of time and place and destiny. [34]

Marble Eye, in whose home Buddy had boarded that weekend, had arrived in Clarendon in 1924. He maintained a flamboyant presence as a flashy dresser with a charismatic personality. He was as active in the civic community affairs of colored town as he was in his own business. In the 1930 US Census he listed his occupation as yard work. There were two versions of how he acquired his nickname. One was that he actually had one prosthetic eye and the other that his eyes were just naturally protruding. His house, a short distance north of the colored school and across the street from the café mentioned by Buddy, centered recreational activities through the years, though there were no overt implications that this involved prostitution. During the weekend that Buddy spent there it was whiskey and a crap game with his two companions. In later years after Prohibition was repealed, Marble Eye's home served as a nightclub where white couples could dance to a jukebox and enjoy mixed drinks. Despite his obvious departure from adherence to the law, he and his home were regarded with respect. As a gesture of that respect from both the black and the white community, a reception was held to celebrate the 50th anniversary of his marriage to his wife, Mary. [35]

The café where Buddy claimed to have encountered the four white boys looking for whiskey and a girl was located at the northwest corner of the area known then as colored town and later as The Flats. On a street map it was North Jefferson Street. The town, two blocks long and two blocks wide, was home to no more than 150 residents. That number was included in the total population of 2000 for the City of Clarendon. [36] That section of colored town had its underground reputation as the location of vice in the area. In 1926 Marble Eye himself had been accused of taking part in a shooting that resulted in his arrest and the serious wounding of Red Wells.[37] This affair appeared to be some kind of turf war. In 1933 Deputy Sheriff Guy Wright lost an eye to a shotgun blast during a raid on another bootlegger, Doc Shoffett, who lived near Marble-Eye's residence. Shoffet paid with a prison sentence. [38] These matters were resolved in a court of law. Clarendon's vice in colored town was policed to the extent that Clarendon could maintain its Saint's Roost image. The threats made by the Ku Klux Klan about bootlegging and prostitution were not enforced but the rape of a white woman was a different matter.

Buddy's short time in Clarendon was sandwiched in between his release on Vagrancy charges in Beloit, Wisconsin on October 11, 1938, his train journey from there and enough time spent picking cotton to earn the wages that he brought to spend at Marble Eye's. The Clarendon Sheriff stated that it was little more than a week.[39] During that time it seems that he wanted to superimpose his Chicago ways upon the North Jefferson Street scene. The girl did not appear to fear the Chicago style of retaliation for "evading the tax" - a savage beating or worse, or she believed she could outsmart Buddy. If truly a Clarendon girl, her protection rested in her community and not in a street pimp in front of the café. Buddy's flamboyant story of the "asparine cigarette" did not belong to this scene either. In that time folkloric tales of a magic buzz resulting from aspirin being mixed with Coke were common in Clarendon but these were things that parents joked about in the presence of their children.[40] In 1938 there were white powdery substances such as heroin, cocaine or PCP that when smoked in a cigarette might have caused the intoxication as described by Buddy. They were readily available on the streets of Chicago where he lived, but the likelihood that a tall, dark stranger bearing such drugs passing them out on North Jefferson Street in Clarendon, Texas, is highly unlikely. But he carried this story with him into the confines of the Texas State Death Row. There no story, no appeal counted.

As in that time, logical minds continue to search for logical explanations for the forces that operate beyond the reach of logic. Drug or alcohol intoxication, unmodulated workings of an intellectually disabled/brain damaged mind or the behavioral norms of a culture of cruelty such as the underworld of Chicago in 1938 defy logic. At that moment in time the sudden explosion of Buddy's cruelty at the dump grounds was as alien to the Clarendon scene as the fantasy of an invader from outer space was to the rest of the nation. In a moral sense for Clarendon it was a war between two worlds.

11

The Potter's Hand

"They sneer at me for leaning all awry:
What! Did the Hand then of the Potter shake?"

THE RUBAIYAT, OMAR KHAYYAM

BUDDY ARRIVED AT Huntsville on November 9 after his last visit with his family. His fate was now in the hands of The Texas Prison System. He had been tried in a court of law, found guilty and sentenced to die for his crime. He had waived his right to appeal. His only hope was the issue of his feeblemindedness, the cause for which his Robertson County neighbors would rally around his mother in an appeal to the Board of Pardons and Parole. This condition of his humanity that evoked compassion among his neighbors evaded recognition at Huntsville.

In 1938 there appear to have been no statutory standards to specifically define "mental abnormalities or "mental incapacity." In a broader sense insanity was defined under the M'Naghten Rules, under which he had been tried. "The M'Naughten Rules, as articulated by the British House of Lords were:

"The jurors ought to be told in all cases that every man is to be presumed to be sane, and to possess a sufficient degree of reason to be responsible for his crimes, until the contrary be proved to their satisfaction; and that to establish a defense on the ground of insanity, it must be clearly proved that, at the time of the committing of the act, the party was laboring under such a defect of reason, from the disease of the mind, as not to know the nature of the act he was doing; or, if he did know it, that he did not know he was doing what was wrong." [1]

For Buddy the matter of legal insanity had been determined at the trial level. His defense had the burden of raising the issue before trial and they had not. It is assumed, then, that in his opening statement to the jury the judge, in compliance with the M'Naghten Rule, had told them to presume him to be of sound mind and capable of understanding the nature of his crime and that it was wrong. Buddy had signed a written confession admitting the crime and his victim fully corroborate the facts in the confession. He waived his right to appeal, and even if he had been found to be insane in the prison, the statutes would have required that he be sent back to the custody of the Donley County sheriff to arrange for commitment to an asylum. [2] The psychiatric services needed for this process were not readily available in the Panhandle before the trial or after sentencing. Holding Morris Norman in a local jail long enough for psychiatric evaluation before or after trial was a threat to his safety and to that of the community. The outcome of the Board of Pardons and Parole's decision was quite predictable. The nature of his crime would seal his fate. [3] In that context it followed that there was no mention of mental incapacity before and during his trial and for that time it escaped mention on death row.

When Morris Norman was committed to Huntsville in 1938, Governor Allred's reform of the Prison System was in its infancy. The nucleus of that reform was the newly formed Bureau of Classification. What had been the subject of a research project for the University of Texas Social Science Department became a merger of sociology and psychology with criminology in the formation of the bureau. It's primary objective: "the judicious segregation and rehabilitation of the inmates upon a scientific and common basis." Implementation of that objective was "to be accomplished through employing the services of trained experts. . . , to examine into the character and mental qualifications of the prisoners as they come into the prison, with a view of placing each in such line of work, and at such unit, wherein the best of the moral and mental characteristics may develop." On Death Row it served to provide a comprehensive summary of each inmate for the consideration of an appeal or plea for clemency. Within days Buddy's family and neighbors were receiving letters from the Classification Officer.[4]

In the Texas Prison System classification and psychiatry would interface in the person of Dr. Abe Hauser. He had served as one of the scientific advisors in that University of Texas project. As the first physician to enter the practice of psychiatry from the University of Texas Medical Branch in Galveston, he was also the first psychiatrist to serve in the Prison System. He played a key role in the development of mental services for The Bureau of Classification and as a result, the system would endorse basic concepts of psychiatry of that time. [5]

Psychiatry of that era was dominated by scientific psychology. Based on Freud's theory of the Id, Ego, and Superego as the developing stages of the human psyche, the scientific approach relied upon deterministic laws of science to explain and manage human behavior. To obtain understanding of the human being and to explain his behavior, the scientific approach focused upon genetic makeup, the largely ungovernable urges of the unconscious mind and upon an analyzation of his observable behaviors. It seemed logical to incorporate these principles into the prison system as a better means of understanding and controlling the inmate population.[6]

All persons committed to prison were first brought to the classification unit and carried through what was called the Bertillon routine – photographed, fingerprinted, measured and asked for biographical data that included family history, occupation, previous criminal and legal history, date of birth, height, weight, race, complexion, eyes, hair, marital status, scars, and general remarks. After a preliminary medical examination and background check was completed, this information was assembled into a folder and the prisoner was ready for interview by the director of the Bureau of Classification or by his assistant. During this interview the prisoner gave his version of his criminal offense and any other personal information having bearing on his situation. After this initial interview, further investigation was conducted by correspondence with the Federal Bureau of Investigation, judicial and law enforcement officials, social service agencies, family members, previous employers and other institutions or sources indicated by the individual's case. [7]

"If during the interview or subsequent investigation any doubt about the inmate's mental status arises, he is referred to the psychiatrist and for a psychometric examination, and his treatment and classification is modified in accordance with these findings. The Army Alpha and Beta tests are used in cases given psychometric examination. Due to limited staff, second interviews have been given only when a special problem made it necessary." [8]

Buddy was given such an interview. At least his condition was noted. The notes taken by the psychiatrist, Dr. Abe Hauser, and his evaluation of them were included in his Classification file but access to the actual document, because it is a medical record, has been denied this writing.[9] Buddy had qualified for the second interview but despite the multiple references to his feeble-mindedness and evidence of it in his history, his mental incapacity was disregarded in the summary of his case. [10]

Dr. Hauser's psychiatric interview was quoted as saying that during the interview no gross personality defects were noted and that there were was no psychosis or mental abnormalities. Dr. Coles' letter of December 5 contained the only direct quote to that effect. As the prison physician, his statement fulfilled the statutory requirements for evaluations by two qualified mental health professions. [11]

The Classification demonstration program had convinced its authors of the need to isolate the insane or intellectually disabled from the main population as they represented a higher level of aggressive behaviors and required a different kind of supervision. During its first year of operation after being approved by the 1937 Legislature the Bureau of Classification was so convinced of this need that the 1938 called session superseded the standards to specify a specific classification for the insane and feebleminded and requirements for their separate housing.[12] So, if there was any question about mental status or the existence of "feeble-mindedness" after sentencing and admission to the prison in the general prison population, the prisoner was given an Affidavit of Insanity evaluation by the warden or prison physician and assigned to the appropriate housing.[13] For death row inmates the psychiatric evaluation had little purpose. For unclear reasons feeble-mindedness or mental illness on death row would have little or no effect upon clemency from the Board of Pardons and Parole decision. In 1938 intellectual disability rarely exempted one from death eligibility. Throughout the history of execution by electrocution only 15 inmates were extended clemency for mental incapacity.[14] Obviously, it did not affect where death row inmates would be housed and evidently did not classify as a "mental abnormality," the words used by both Dr. Cole and Dr. Hauser to disqualify mental incapacity. With this evaluation of his mental capacities referencing Dr. Hauser's December 9, 1938 psychiatric interview and the December 5, 1938 letter written by Dr. Cole:

"I have examined the above captioned inmate this morning and do not see any abnormality. He seems to be the average negro.
Trusting this is the information desired, I am:
Respectively,
T. C. Cole, M. D., Medical Supervisor [15]

The issue of intellectual disability or feeble-mindedness," as it was called at that time, factored little in criminal responsibility, only in matters of housing placement. The psychometric testing used by the Bureau of Classification to measure inmate intelligence was the Army Alpha and Beta developed by Robert Yerkes at the beginning of World War I.[16]

This test was originally developed to meet the demands for a systematic method of evaluating the intellectual and emotional functioning of soldiers. Hastily formulated to meet an immediate demand, the test was originally designed for group testing. The procedures were later expanded to accommodate the foreign speaking and illiterate recruits and to point out the feeble-minded incapable of military service. Inherent in the conditions surrounding its creation and premises upon which it was based, the test proved to be flawed to the extent that it was abandoned by the Army after World War I. [17]

By 1936, when the Texas Prison System classification demonstration was initiated, the test had been revised with improvements and specific adjustment of norms for use with civilian populations. Its immediate availability and its appeal to accomplish a similar need for classification for a population such as served by The Texas Prison System its adoption for use by the Bureau of Classification seemed appropriate. But sadly, flaws in the Army Alpha and Beta introduced a negative form of thinking that would haunt The Texas Prison System for decades, especially so in the way it fostered stereotypical discrimination of race and class.[18] In his comprehensive study of the death penalty in Texas, Marquart commented that this racial bias was the product of Jim Crow thinking. Guthrie expressed his view of the racism in the title of his historical review of Scientific Psychology, *Even the Rat Was White*. The very process of classification of prisoners was judgmental. It had to take into account an inmate's past history of behavior and moral decisions. It had to underline weaknesses and areas with poor prognosis. The reliance in psychiatry of that time upon diagnosis via personality defects, fairly enduring patterns of inner experience and behavior that bring a person into repeated conflict with society, and maladaptive defense mechanisms added a negative tone to its evaluations.[19]

In his zeal to establish intelligence testing as a hard science, the principle author of the Army Alpha testing had believed that his tests measured "native intellectual ability" and that this was a fixed value unaffected by culture and educational opportunities. Early evaluation of such IQ testing noted that cultural and racial minorities consistently scored lower on the test. This provided the opportunity for some scholars of that time to justify the notion that this was due to the genetic inferiority of the minorities and not to flaws in the testing. Resonating with scientific emphasis at that time on "nature over nurture" the expanded uses of intelligence testing led to the accepted scientific belief that race and socioeconomic strata equated to levels of intelligence.[20] Some scientist using these "facts" to justify eugenics and the notion of racial superiority of Northern Europeans actually affected national immigration policies in the United States and ultimately inspired the policies of "racial purity" used by the Nazis to justify their genocide of the Jews.[21]

Today's reader is startled by some of the wording used in the Classification Summary of Buddy, others outraged by the description of him and the conclusions drawn from the psychiatric evaluation that were sent to the board of Pardons and Parole.[22] Understood in context of the standards in place at that time and setting can one be grateful for a system of law that checks the excesses of cruelty with the standards of decency that have evolved. We can be both gravely concerned and hopeful for those that have not.

In the psychiatry of that time standardized diagnoses as we have today were not in use. Impressions were discussed more in terms of personality defects and a hierarchy of defense mechanisms ranked higher and lower, adaptive to maladaptive. The mental status examination used by the Prison System in the Classification Summary, because of the purpose it was intended to serve, was limited as a true mental status evaluation. Entitled "Personality," it followed a modified format containing only General Appearance, Attitude and Behavior and with that information directed toward meeting the needs of classification. Things emphasized under appearance were detailed descriptions of distinguishing features, race and color – detailed with comments on the shades of that color, ebony-skinned negro, negro with copper complexion, light skinned Mexican. Description of an inmate served as a verbal mug shot for identification purposes. Emphasis was also placed on the description of build in a manner suggestive of his aptitude for manual labor – "heavy-set," "husky youth," "tall, well-built, muscular," "rather thin." [23] Impressions were often given in a judgmental manner reflecting more the biases of the evaluator and to serve the purposes of classification than the true mental state of the inmate.

The inmate's attitude was usually taken from a list of terms used in the standard mental status examination but comments on motor activity, speech, emotional state, thought processes, intelligence, fund of knowledge and adaptive functioning were not given with objective data but lumped into racial and socio-economic categories and a hierarchy of maladaptive defense mechanisms. These were explained away with stereotypical beliefs applied to them. [24] In that Texas prison setting all of the negative scientific, psychiatric and social biases of that era were gathered into an inmate's "Personality" summary.

In Western Europe studies in psychiatry were promoting the belief that origins of psychiatric disease were biological and predominately genetic. Resonating with the "science of intelligence testing" theories and the pseudo research that followed that school of thought, psychiatry began to embrace theories of "genetic hygiene" and to champion social Darwinism. This social movement challenged the compassionate gestures of more child centered educational theories and welfare relief systems such as those in Chicago as threats to undermine the biological "struggle for survival" inherent in the processes of natural selection. The psychiatric diagnosis based on this so called scientific assumption was criticized even by its own as appearing to be a list of undesirable behaviors, the personality disorders. In the beginning these were known as ways to describe "moral insanity" as distinguished from the delusions or hallucinations seen in psychosis. The belief in the "born criminal" in that era was predominant. Deterrents to crime, then, were seen in a hierarchy of punishments befitting the crime for the criminal and "genetic hygiene" for society.[25]

In 1938 The Texas Prison System provided a unique setting for these emerging beliefs to flourish. The Old Southern notion of white supremacy still reigned and quite readily resonated with theories promoting its genetic superiority. In an agrarian culture "genetic hygiene" was routinely practiced with pruning and culling.

"Descriptions of the condemned offenders . . . provide a glimpse into the beliefs and practices of the day:

The subject is a husky youth of average stature, red-haired, frank in attitude, serious of mien, whose general behavior is that of a town-dwelling youth of better than average laborer's level. His history would seem to indicate that he is an amoral youth capable of vicious behavior.

Subject is an average-sized, ebony skin, well-built Negro, with a rather bullet-shaped head and prominently Negroid features. His vocabulary is consistent with his reported grammar school education and his mannerisms are those of the average urban Negro laborer.

Subject is an average-sized, well-built, rather good-looking Mexican youth, with a skin which is lighter than the average run of Mexicans. His vocabulary and language are poor, and his stock of knowledge is limited, as is consistent with his reported Mexican labor background."

"The subject is a rather small, but strongly built, heavy-set negro with dark skin. He assumes the attitude of the urban, sophisticated, negro play-boy, but his thought process, language and vocabulary are those of a person of limited education and background. During his ten years of living in Corpus Christi, he apparently picked up a good many surface tricks of speech and manner of the urban sophisticate, but the adjustment never went very deep and his manner is quite unconvincing. During the interview he assumed a suave, sailing, devil-may-care attitude and his story was replete with quips, wisecracks and indefinite answers. However, he was quite nervous and this seemed to be a device to keep up his courage." [26]

So it is that Buddy's mental status was described:

"The subject is a rather tall, slender, but well-built individual, with ebony-black skin, rather stolid features and undemonstrative expression.

During the interview, he was very nervous, but assumed an attitude of co-operation, although he encountered difficulty in remembering and spelling names. His vocabulary and language are limited and his mannerisms are those of the average tenant farm negro. His history indicates that he is an unstable individual who has been unable to adjust adequately to his home environment, to accepting and holding steady employment, or to his term in the Civilian Conservation Corps. . . . He rationalizes his present offense, first in terms of his innocence, and second in terms of his intoxication and the effect of the doped cigarette." [27]

Buddy, as the others, was evaluated by his race, level of socioeconomic status, personality defects, coping mechanisms and level of adaptation to his environment - the standard measures of scientific psychology.

Determination of criminal responsibility of the "feebleminded" was not defined in 1938. Whether his historically obvious intellectual disabilities, mentioned several times in the Classification Summary, were noted in the psychiatric interview cannot be known. There are questions about the accuracy of the summary of his evaluation of Buddy written by the Classification Officer or at least doubt that it reflected all that was noted by the doctor. Buddy's Inmate File contains four pages of psychiatric notes plus the official evaluation. Buddy's condition could not have escaped the doctor's attention.[28] That it totally escaped notation raise perplexing questions even for today. In 1938 there was no legal standard in place to acknowledge the matter of Buddy's mental incapacity. It was more expedient to explain it away with the jargon of the so called scientific psychology of that time.

12

Explaining Buddy

And so these men of Indostan
Disputed loud and long
Each in his opinion
Exceeding stiff and strong
Though each was partly in the right,
And all were in the wrong! . . .
Rail on in utter ignorance
Of what each other mean,
And prate about an elephant
Not one of them has seen.

JOHN GODFREY SAXE

WITHIN THE SYSTEMIC confines of Death Row the means to explain Buddy's limitations or to address them with more compassion were not available. The data collected by the Classification officials within the time span of one month contained a remarkably comprehension social and medical history. In another setting whose purpose had been the rehabilitation and restoration of Buddy into society, it could have served to develop quite a different clinical assessment.

The description of his appearance in itself would have alerted an evaluator to abnormalities as it did the Chicago Traveler's Aid worker. She noted "a noticeable scar running lengthwise on the forehead," a clue to possible etiology of his expressionless face. In the physical examination performed for the Classification Summary the scar was described in detail in medical shorthand but not referred to in the Classification Summary. His mug shots showed not only the scar on his forehead but a turkey track scar running from it across his entire right temple. This would have justified further medical and social history investigation to determine the extent of this head injury and its pathological consequences. Another long scar at the base of his neck was suggestive of a knife wound scar and called for further medical examination for body scars suggestive of physical abuse and violence and its contribution to his aggressive behaviors. [1]

Buddy's blank expressionless face had engendered a wide range of interpretations. The Classification Summary called it "stolid." Panhandle newspapers described him as "smug, pretentious," "smug and cold-blooded . . He did not show the slightest emotion or fear until he was taken into the court room," "Smugness ends" as he heard the jury's verdict. "The cold blooded negro made his first show of emotion."

Robertson County neighbors who saw him grow up commented that they never saw him smile in his life. They commonly saw him standing beside the road looking bewildered and lost. None, but the Chicago Aid's worker, acknowledged the severe wound to his head which might have robbed his face of the ability to show emotion and in turn deprived his internal capacity for emotion and social judgment.

His nervousness was reported by the press to have been noticeable when he was brought into the courtroom and when his verdict was read. At that time the Amarillo reporter wrote that he verbalized fear of mob action and of not being able to see his mother again. Noting that in stressful situations – when he was brought into the court room, when he heard the verdict, when he was interviewed by the Classifications Officer - Buddy consistently appeared noticeably shaken suggests other possibilities - fear of harm in novel situations, psychomotor excitements indicative of inner tensions, and/or of several pathologies. It could have signaled an immature or autistic level of functioning or PTSD resulting from his childhood abuse. The Classifications Officer dismissed it by saying that "he assumed an attitude of cooperation."

His distinctive speech was noted as "limited language and vocabulary" by the prison and "speaking in a slow stuttering fashion with vague content" by the Aid worker. A Calvert banker stated that he never talked with good sense. Notations of his speech patterns and content are glaring clues to his pathology. They point both to the head injury and to the level of his intelligence. A sensitive Aid's worker observed the speech deficits. Biased by Buddy's race and the nature of his crime, others ignored or explained them away. Excerpts from his confession and side comments in the courtroom were mentioned by the local press. Letters from local representatives of law enforcement gave details of his confession of "lurid acts," and the Memphis Democrat broke the story of his "asparine cigarette" but no mention was made of his manner of speaking by any of these sources. The Classification Summary noted his limited vocabulary and ability to communicate but stated this was because he was the average negro tenant farmer.

The Aid's worker documented some of Buddy's behavioral characteristics as though she was knowledgeable of research being conducted at that time in some Midwestern Universities into the link between childhood brain injuries in the area of the forehead and a pattern of personality traits that also seemed to be associated with aberrant behaviors. Known as the Case of JP these scientists hoped to establish a documented syndrome of these traits seen in victims of childhood prefrontal lobe trauma such as in the young man known as JP. These were a persistent tendency to wander, superficial politeness with adults, inappropriate boastfulness, denial of wrongdoing with elaborate excuses, excitement seeking behaviors, inability to hold a job, impulsivity and social isolation.

The Aid's worker recorded his story about arriving in Chicago aboard a barnstorming airplane. The next day a Chicago social worker documented his boast about being rodeo performer. Throughout the body of the social history assembled by the Classification Officers were references to his roving, elaborate excuses for wrongdoing, excitement seeking, inability to hold a job and the impulsivity that earned him the nickname of "Must Have It" by his peers. Before authority figures he was said to be cooperative and "humble."

The frontal lobe area of the brain, located at the forehead, is the center of reasoning or so called executive functioning. It is as though it is the switchboard to all other areas of the brain that store information, gather sensory data and facilitate physical and intellectual activity. At the console of the frontal lobe one normally could connect jacks to one or many of these sources at the same time and quickly synthesize a reasoned response.

Inability to hold steady employment as one of the behaviors under study at the time Buddy entered the Chicago Relief system, had an understandable scientific explanation. Deprived of normal executive thinking by the possibility of brain damage caused by the Whooping Cough and a more documented injury to the frontal lobe area of his brain, he lacked the ability to conceptualize a task or to plan the steps necessary for achieving it. To his father, the son of a slave, this trait no doubt represented laziness for which the punishment was a beating. With cerebral functioning for survival more at his command he developed skills for avoiding punishment with elaborately contrived rationalizations.

A letter from a Calvert banker and merchant wrote poignant details of Buddy's roving:

"I found him on several occasions in nearby towns wanting to come home. He didn't seem to know where he had been – just gotten a ride and wanted to go home." [2]

Another banker and merchant added a pertinent example of his limited capacity for abstract reasoning.

"He was in my dry goods store one day to buy a pair of shoes but had to leave because he had no means of paying for them. In less than an hour, he was back with a five dollar bill and said a man had just given it to him and that he thought he better come get the shoes while he had the money. On investigation, I found the manager of my grocery department had sent him with the bill to the bank for change. He readily admitted the incident but said he did not know what change meant at the bank and he had rather have the shoes" [3]

A standard Mental Status Exam technique for evaluating frontal lobe - executive functioning or capacity for abstract thought - is through the use of the proverb such as seen in this story. An adult of average or nearly average intelligence is capable of abstract thinking. If a client is unable to give abstract responses to a proverb, organic brain disease, schizophrenia or intellectual disability should be suspected.

His capacity for reasoning was at the level of a child. He understood the cause and effect relationship between a five dollar bill and a pair of shoes but he could not conceptualize the sequence of actions involved in taking the bill to the bank, getting change and returning it to the grocery store. Had he actually been given change for the bill, at this level of reasoning, he might have believed that now he had five bills instead of one so he could buy five pairs of shoes. Or simply that he wanted the shoes so he must have them.

Aside from the "asparine cigarette story" that he added later, Buddy told the Classification Officer that he used alcohol and that he had been drunk before the attack (and the cigarette), another problematic pattern of behavior. All local sources denied his intoxication, possibly because the matter of intoxication could have compromised prosecution's request for the death penalty. It was reported to the Press that when he was first apprehended he was found to be sleeping soundly. The Texas Ranger represented his sleepiness as a lack of remorse, stating that after signing the confession he fell asleep on the way to the Amarillo jail at 5:30 a.m. With a psychiatric understanding of how alcohol, even in small amounts, can have an exaggerated effect upon injured brain tissue this fact could have added to a possible understanding of his behaviors during the attack. In his history there were two reports of arrests involving alcohol, one in Robertson County for "disorderly drinking" and in Chicago for "drunkenness." In retrospect it seems one of the more plausible explanations for the sudden and atypical outburst of violence. [4]

The sudden changes experienced after prefrontal lobe injury in an adult was generally known and often referred to as a frontal lobe personality through the famous case of Phineas Gage in 1848. Mr. Gage, a railroad worker, had suffered a significant head injury. A long spike had entered and exited through the forehead of his skull. Immediately afterwards the friends of Phineas Gage commented that he just was "not Gage" any more." He was more angry and aggressive, could not remember or plan things as well and, once a quiet and reserved individual, now continuously "entertained" his friends with inappropriate humor and endless stories. One scientist discussing the differences between behavioral changes due to frontal lobe injuries in adults and children noted that Phineas Gage was examined by a Harvard professor and declared normal. The fact that he "simply was not Gage anymore" defied measurement. [5]

The research initiated by the case of JP sought to explain why these dramatic changes did not seem to be notable in children at the time of the injury but manifest and enduring as they matured. They seemed to "grow into impairments" more detrimental than those seen in adults with similar injuries. Children deprived of integration of skills derived from frontal lobe processing of social cognitions and exchanges of facial expressions during their formative years often emerge from adolescence with outbursts of aberrant behaviors not seen before.[6] In her studies of brain damaged juveniles and a pattern of "purposeless aggression" Dr. Dorothy Lewis spotlighted childhood neglect and abuse as a strong factor. [7]

Confusing to stereotypical understandings of mental incapacity, those caused prefrontal lobe pathology are not global. Memory functions and perceptual motor skills are sometimes spared. Even though he had been deprived of education and was reputedly incapable of it, for the social worker for Travelers Aid in Chicago, the Texas Rangers in their Clarendon interrogation and the Classification Officer in the Huntsville prison, he could recall specific dates, names and addresses. Even though the officer commented that Buddy had difficulty remembering and spelling the names of his Robertson County neighbors, he communicated them well enough that 14 letters were mailed to them from the Classification office on November 11, 1938, two days after his arrival in Huntsville. [8]

He could not have named the capitals of three states for intelligence testing, but he could have found the train that took him to them. Without the benefit of literate understanding of letters and numbers his mind contained the maps and the ability to remember them. He knowledgeably discussed the routes of his highway and train journeys with the Chicago Travelers worker and the Texas Classification Officer. He retraced the routing and timing of his train ride from Beloit, Wisconsin, to the Clarendon area. He also had the ability to contrive dates to advantage as he did with the Travelers Aid worker in order to meet their criteria for entitlement. He changed his story about arriving to the Chicago area with the barnstorming pilot by saying that he was dropped off without pay only the day before and "had been walking the streets of Chicago" since. This indicated that he knew the Aid's entitlement criteria required that clients must be homeless and in Chicago no more than three weeks.

Buddy's Ranger press agent might have classified this coping skill as "cunning." The Classification Summary called his social adaptation "unstable" and "poor." Forced to fend for himself, he had learned coping skills and those included "working the relief system." He had a good sense of geography. He had highwayed through his world since childhood and traveled the railroads in his youth.

In the humanistic approach things such as these are seen as strengths and an effort would be made to enhance them and utilize them to incorporate him into society as a useful participant. The Chicago Aid worker found him shelter in a Newberry House for that November night and referred him the next day to a Relief worker. During the time that he lived in the supportive environment of the shelter and worked for Mr. Gould who praised his work and expressed confidence in him, Buddy apparently fulfilled that role. [9]

Life in The Tree Army could not provide the structure and individual supervision required by his condition. Neither did the CCC have access to a referral system with appropriate options for his placement after leaving them. He was discharged to a boarding house of his choice near the railroad tracks of Beloit, Wisconsin. There he was pulled back into the riptides of the ominous currents of man's cruelty and inhumanity that were circling the globe. He and the compassionate few who reached out to him were defenseless against their forces.

In 1938 the Texas Prison System identified "feeble-mindedness" for the purpose of appropriately housing it, but declined to note it in matters involving death eligibility. It defined intelligence on the basis of race and socioeconomic status. Later it used the scientifically advanced Weschler Intelligence Quotient to define intelligence and a score of 71 to determine criminal responsibility.[10] Three quarters of a century later the Supreme Court struck down the use of an IQ score to define Intellectual disability in capital cases. In June, 2014, Supreme Court Justice Anthony Kennedy wrote, "Intellectual disability is a condition, not a number." [11] One law professor commented: "States will now be required to take a less mechanical approach in capital cases. "Death row inmates suffer from multidimensional mental problems. … Today's ruling requires courts to investigate these fully, by looking at the elephant rather than the tail." [12]

Buddy, expressionless, lost - at the edge of logic.

Today scientists, jurists and society at large continue to grope the elephant. It defies our definitions. We cannot agree upon a static measure of intelligence. We are still unable to measure the fluctuating ability of prefrontal lobes to modulate the animal-like urges of the limbic system or the fluctuating intensities of the limbic system to overpower the modulations of logic. Those who grapple with establishing standards of decency are stalemated on this issue for both the intellectually impaired and the mentally ill. One might have the knowledge of right and wrong or the intellectual capacity to consider consequences of an action in one moment and not in another. [13]

What were the workings of his "feeble mind" and did he deserve death? Within the confines of his mentality what abilities to survive and cope with the world did he have? And in that limited world what standards of decency could he understand, and more importantly, even if he understood them, restrain his impulses to act otherwise? He lashed out impulsively on his rage and sexual arousal but upon hearing the prayers of his victims, helped them to their feet. Before he walked away, he threatened to kill them if they screamed out. Three hours later when brought before them for identification, he rushed to one of them begging for forgiveness. Nine days later he denied the whole thing with his story of the "asparine" cigarette.

We today, even as he was then, are held hostage somewhere between a struggle for decency and the loss of our humanity in the commonality of cruelty. The final judgment rests in the eternal truth that at any level, from the bench to the execution chamber, there is a margin of error in human judgment

13

The Question

*"His feeble mind must have caused him to get into that trouble.
He did a wrong and needs punishment, . . . but does he deserve
death? No, he did not take a life and he should be let live if it
is in a prison or hospital. . . . I am hoping that I may help you
all see some other way than death for him.*

LORENE STEPHENSON[1]

DURING THE TIME Traveler's sojourn to the year 802,701 AD, he la-
mented the descent of mankind with gloom. He had rescued
Little Weena from the uncaring complacency of her fellowmen, the
elite of the upper world, and viewed with dismay the forces of the underworld overcoming mankind with cruelty. As he fortified himself
against the advance of evil, Little Weena danced at his side stuffing
exotic white flowers into his pockets and covering his hands with kisses
of gratitude and tenderness. These had survived the descent of mankind [2]

Bremond, Texas
Nov. 15, 1938

Mr. G. W. Graham,
Huntsville, Texas.

Dear Sir,

In regard to your letter of recent
stating that my name had been given as a
reference by Morris Norman (negro), who has
been sentenced to die Dec. 16.

The above named negro was known
to me as "Buddie Norman", while growing
up here. His family has lived within a few
miles of my home since he was a child.
The family is large, being poor common negroes,
and none of them have been in any trouble
that I know of. I don't think Buddie could learn
anything in school and did not attend long, so
he must have not been intelligent as the case
with many negroes. When he was small, he and
his little brother would come to my home
and play with my brothers toys, as they had nothing. They would ask for things but never stole
anything. We had to tell them when to go home.

After Buddie grew up he roved about a lot
and he and his Dad could not get along, so
he left home. I don't believe they knew

where he was for a long time, or how he got in the C C ccamp. I heard that the family was a happy bunch when they got the first money. One of the little boys said "we are rich now". I had not heard any thing of him until this week, and it was a shock to me to hear what had become of him. His feeble mind must have caused him to get into that trouble. He did a wrong we know and needs punishment, but does he deserve death? No, he did not take a life and he should be let live, if it is in a prison or hospital.

My brother recieved a letter also and he is not here but at Palestine, Texas, Mr. E.R. Stephenson. He would say the same thing I have and that he gave him plenty of dimes that he will not get back from Buddie.

I am hopping that I may help you all see some other way than death for him. (I am a school teacher, attended college at Huntsville this summer, and visited the prison, the ball games and rodeo.)

Very truly yours,
Miss Lorene Stephenson

Written on notebook paper by a 21 year old school teacher and directed to the Board of Pardons and Parole during the forty-six days that Buddy's fate was in their hands, a few simple words represented mankind's latent capacity for tenderness and compassion in a time when scientific elitism and theories of white supremacy were igniting a worldwide holocaust.

Though for 75 years her letter has had few readers, her message has represented the will of the people in stating the agenda for what Chief Justice Earl Warren would call An Evolution of Decency in Constitutional law. "The Eighth Amendment must draw its meaning from the evolving standards of decency that mark the progress of a maturing society." [3]

Typical of a rural community teacher of that time, Lorene Stephenson only had three years of public school education, little more than Buddy. Primarily self-educated, she had already taught that many years. With pride she wrote in her letter about her attendance at Sam Houston University's summer institute for teachers and her visit to the prison at Huntsville. The letter might not have scored high in a college English composition class. It contained several misspelled words, but it was punctuated with caring as she described Buddy as a child.

Always the rover and always in search of adventure, he and his younger brother, Walter, frequently wandered from his shanty home up the road to the Stephenson home where he knew he was welcome to play with the abundance of toys of Lorene's youngest brother, Weldon. Buddy never required discipline, only to be reminded when it was time to go home. Lorene's older brother, Ernest, took pleasure in giving the boys dimes to watch them feel rich and perhaps to enjoy casting his bread upon the waters. As the boys grew old enough to go to the fields their trips to the Stephenson place were discontinued. Community rumors of Buddy's problems with his father explained his departure. Later, word that he had somehow made it to a CCC camp circulated after the community heard about his allotment check. Buddy's little brothers, Harry and Fletcher, spread the word that now they were rich. Lizzie bragged that her son was serving in the Tree Army. Lorene applauded a home town boy's accomplishment, and now she pled for a better way to carry out his punishment. [4]

Changes were already underway in Texas' criminal justice system at the time of Buddy's arrest and trial. The trial itself had represented a victory for law and order in Texas and marked the demise of its shameful legacy of lynching. It marked the beginning of scientific crime investigation. Though Buddy's conviction was based on his confession, a conviction could have easily been substantiated upon other available evidence. Castings of the tell-tale shoe prints leading from the scene of the crime to the shoes found under his bed at Marble Eye's, laboratory analysis of the blood stains left on his clothing, statements from witnesses to his apology to his victim in the living room of the Green home – any one of these, added to the testimony of Cora Ferris, could have convicted him. On the horizon was the day when a confession, with its potentials for abuse and misuse, would not represent the only means of conviction. The teacher's neighbor and part time pastor spoke to this concern: "I believe that he was just a suspicious character and he was scared into saying he was guilty." [5]

On a larger worldwide scale decency was on a rapid decline. Under the guise of improvement for the condition of mankind, scientific psychology, eugenics and social Darwinism had actually promoted racism and genetic cleansing toward a cruelty that paled The Time Traveler's gloomy predictions. The Texas Prison System was caught up that philosophical downward spiral even in the midst of its advances toward modernizing the system. There was no answer to the teacher's question in 1938. There was no other way than death for Buddy. Not until after it had to pass through the inferno of a worldwide holocaust did mankind emerge coated with ashes of penitence that sobered his view of himself. As an unspoken derivative of the eugenics of 1938 that favored selective breeding and genetic cleansing, execution of the intellectually disabled remained acceptable. After the horrors of World War II, ideas of genetic cleansing were repugnant but the death penalty, without regard for mental incapacities, remained unchanged.

Breaking the bondage of class and white supremacy that still re-mained in the South, it was the Civil Rights movement that finally sparked the Evolution of Decency in the Supreme Court.

The Miranda rights, 1966, addressed abuses of the confession to thwart rights to a fair trial. At the time of Buddy's arrest these were not standards to even consider. Acquiring a confession as early as possible was the chief aim of law enforcement and the use of it by the prosecu-tion was a primary source of evidence. "You have the right to remain silent. Anything you say can and will be used against you in the court of law. You have the right to an attorney. If you cannot afford an attorney, one will be provided for you. Do you understand the rights I have just read to you? With these rights in mind, do you wish to speak to me?" [6]

In 1972 the *Furham v. Georgia* decision challenged the "wanton, ar-bitrary and capricious" imposition of the death penalty as cruel and un-usual punishment. "The discretion for imposing death sentencing must provide objective criteria to direct and limit it and ensured it appellant review." In speaking for the majority Justice Stewart actually stated that he believed that Furman was sentenced to die for his crime because he was a black man. [7]

Though in 1977 the death penalty was reinstated, *Coker V. Georgia*, it now excluded it as a penalty for rape. "Imposing the death sentence for the crime of rape is out of proportion to the crime." [8]

As a spokesman for compassion for the mentally ill the teacher's plea would wait a quarter of a century before it was heard in the halls of criminal justice. There it remained imprisoned within the confines of the dictums of scientific psychology while the blind men groped that tail. What was happening in the main body of modern science was be-yond their grasp.

The research team who first published the case of JP in 1942 con-tinued its search into the unexplained regions of aberrant behaviors in young people. In trying to pinpoint evidence of brain trauma they pointed other researchers with the advanced technology capable of pin-pointing the damage toward the bewildering complexity of newfound knowledge regarding possible additional etiologies for the damage. The most perplexing of these was evidence of the impact of human neglect and abuse upon the brain of a child. Through neuroimaging young brains subjected to traumatic experiences, Dr. Bruce Perry discovered that neglect or sensory deprivation imposed actual organic injury and caused deficits in mental development. The studies he conducted on young victims of all kinds of traumatic experiences including the Columbine High School shootings and the Oklahoma City bombings provided insight into the mysteries of where this ever growing menace of violent behaviors was coming from, but it raised more serious questions about the ominous implications it held for future human development. Perry and others discovered that the impact of traumatic experiences on the child not only thwarted his normal neurodevelopment but inhibited the present functioning of the DNA potentials so that his genetic legacy would be affected. "This has ominous implications for human development." [9]   Today criminologists and forensic psychologists confirm the findings of the neuroscientists:

"...recent research has suggested that when life experiences influence genetic expression, these genetic changes might also be passed on to offspring, (Weinhold, 2006), possibly resulting in a next generation genetically predisposed to having similar cognitions and behaviors." [10]

There are echoes of the Time Traveler's words about the evolution of cruelty, "The inhuman sons of men ... Very inhuman, you may think, to want to go killing one's own descendants! ..." He felt hate for the cruelty of those of the underworld but concern for the latent cruelty within his own heart. In one hand he held a weapon but in the other he held Little Weena. [11]

The research on prison management of the intellectually disabled as presented in Classification in the Texas Prison System published the day before Buddy's execution in 1938 acknowledge the relationship of intellectual disability upon criminality. Criminologists in prison systems were responding to the teachers opening sentence – "His feeble mind must have caused him to get into that trouble." From ancient times when it was called "moral insanity" to 1938 to the present, the realities of criminality among the intellectually disabled remain apparent. The humanistic approach to psychology and criminology edged forward until it was finally expressed in the 2002 Supreme Court's decision in *Atkins v. Virginia* that abolished execution of the mentally disabled.

Justice Stevens in his opinion in *Atkins v. Virginia said*:

"Those mentally retarded persons who meet the law's requirements for criminal responsibility should be tried and punished when they commit crimes. Because they may be less able to give meaningful assistance to their counsel, are typically poor witnesses and their demeanor may create an unwarranted impression of lack of remorse for their crimes, in the aggregate they face a special risk of wrongful execution. The Court rules that execution of a mentally retarded person is deemed 'cruel and unusual punishment.'"[12]

The law's ability to define that state remained with the blind men yet another decade.

The use of an arbitrary IQ score of 70 to define it was struck down in *Hall v. Florida*, in 2014. Justice Anthony Kennedy declared, "Intellectual Disability is a condition not a number."[13] This represented a large step toward reconciling the differences between the sciences and the law in their respective views of mental disability and criminal responsibility. The strict right wing jurists hold that the Constitution is not responsible for an evolution of decency and imply that science cannot change its mind as it advances. The more liberal view is that the very principles that created the Constitution bring these things into harmony over time.

Criminologists of today acknowledge the correlation between childhood abuse and neglect as well as intellectual disabilities upon criminality and they advocate ways to prevent it. "Give these children at the level of their capacities opportunities to learn essential life coping skills – communication, emotional regulation, social skills and In Lorene's simple words in 1938, "a way other than death." They underlined the need to prevent the criminality by giving sense of efficacy, significance and when possible, job skills. [14] We cannot expect life on the streets to sustain their needs. Roving the country by train hopping and walking the streets of Chicago surely sealed Buddy's ultimate destiny. Within every one of the hundreds of death row inmate files secured in the archives of the State Library rests a human story - of a crime, its victims and all the lives caught up in it. And every one of these criminals was once a child.

Left with the regrets of what might have been, awed by all that was caught up in the swirl that descended onto the dump ground in Clarendon in 1938 we emerge with what, blended and distilled, is Well's 4th dimension, that which endures. We face what may be. The predictions of the epigenesist can be terrifying. Or, when seen in the context of its probable causes, it may be hope inspiring. The genetic structure of children exposed to neglect, abuse and violent surroundings is altered and therefore passed on as altered. The chilling predictions of a science fiction writer of another century become the valid scientific concerns of today: Lorene's hope for some other way, Little Weena's gift of flowers for the heart of mankind, a new breed of eugenicist, all suggest that the destiny of the human species may in large measure rest in the way we nurture our young. Science's understanding of his weak mind has circled through theories of genetic cleansing, genetic manipulation and judgmental dictums back to the infant cradled on the pillow in Lizzie's lap.

What were the legacies that had placed him there and what forces would form his sustenance beyond the pillow?

14

Mother's There, Expecting Me

W ESLEY AND LIZZIE Norman were typical of the first generation Freed Men that congregated into Texas. Prior to the Civil War there was a steady migration westward from the Old South of men interested in growing and marketing cotton on new land. The Brazos River Valley in Robertson County was a magnet that attracted them. They brought their slaves with them as well as farm implements, seed, and the tools for plantation operation. The first arrivals took land west of the Little Brazos Valley and what is now Hearne. Since both of Lizzie's parents, Morris and Mittie Turner, were born in Texas in 1857 and 1867 and she was born in Burleson County in 1888 it is likely that they were a part of this migration. [1]

The Robertson County plantations flourished. Enterprising railroad builders began extending lines toward Hearne. Planters increased their production. Though the outbreak of the Civil War stalled the railroads, it intrigued the planters with a dream of an empire of Southern States. The people of Robertson County enthusiastically supported the Southern cause. Two-thirds of the male population joined the Confederate Army and left for war. [2]

When the Civil War was over, the Brazos Valley veterans returned to the land. They left a third of their number dead and some who returned were wounded. To fill the resulting manpower shortage plantation own-ers sent agents to North Carolina recruiting Negro laborers by the car-load. The black population of Hearne swelled.[3] In the late 1880's this included Wesley Norman, his parents and some of his younger siblings from Upper Fishing Creek, North Carolina. From that time on the two families, Normans and Turners, lived in close proximity in the Hearne area though Lizzie and Wesley did not marry until around 1913.[4]

The two families, both Baptists, were likely also together in the black Baptist church of Hearne known as The Little Flock Church. Dating back to the 1870's when the blacks began their mass migration west-ward through the wilderness and bitter cold winter they found shelter and spiritual sanctuary in the building originally built as a hospital for railroad workers and later set aside for the black community. There they flocked together, thus giving the church the name it still bears. [5]

At the time that Morris Norman, third child of Wesley and Lizzie, was born, being a black in Hearne, Texas carried some prestige. Buddy spent the first four years of his childhood in the Hearne community. During those years plantation farming had remained. Wesley enjoyed the status of a rent farmer. [6] The Hearne community boasted a popula-tion of blacks equal to or larger than that of the white population. As a result of the Reconstruction days many of the blacks from Hearne had engaged in Austin politics and others had risen to the status of educated professional men. Black men numbered among the successful merchants and businessmen of the area. [7]

Blacks were also included in those several doctors that served the community. Concern for public health issues in Hearne was advanced for the time due largely to the influence of pioneer Dr. Cummings. As a leader in the Texas Medical Association he championed the cause of public health. [8]

There was adequate medical care for Lizzie's baby in Hearne, but it does not appear that it was accessed. Firstly, babies of that time were at the mercy of whooping cough for the lack of protection against it. The Pertussis vaccine was not developed until the 1930's. The disease in such a young infant was dangerous and the consequences that Lizzie described for the Classification Summary were possible, failure to thrive and brain damage due to deprivation of oxygen. Statistically, these consequences were rare. [9] The bigger puzzle was the fall from the swing. For some reason it appears that Lizzie minimized that injury in favor of the whooping cough as the cause of Buddy's "weak mind." This belief was also reflected in the letters from her neighbors. [10]

The scar that Buddy carried on his forehead and right temple throughout his life bore witness to the fact that the wound received no emergency treatment. The scar was jagged across the forehead and spread across his right temple in a ragged untamed turkey track. The wound had not been sutured. Transportation from the farm to Hearne or even ignorance about such treatment might have prevented access to this care. Lack of knowledge about the effects of head injuries when she did know about the consequences of whooping cough may have made it simpler for her to blame the known. Even so, nagging unanswered questions remain. In the presence of her husband Lizzie completely denied the matter of Buddy's need for punishment to the social worker, "Easy to control and did not receive severe punishment at home," she stated. The beatings Buddy received from his father were referred to in many of the letters written by her neighbors. Mail carrier, R.H. Stellbauer, wrote, "I have been told that he left home because his father whipped him so terribly hard." That he did not get along with his father was the consensus in the letters for why he left home. Lizzie explained that he left home looking for work. And for some reason she, the neighbors and Buddy all recalled that the date was May, 1937.[11]

Three major floods visited the Brazos Valley from 1899 to1921. The one that occurred in the fall of 1921 was so devastating that the heavy rains so engorged the Brazos River that it "ran backwards for miles" overflowing into the Little Brazos River in the Hearne area. Losses to the railroads, farms and livestock put an end to the era of plantations in the area.[12] Before the next farming season Wesley relocated his family to Franklin when Buddy was four and Walter, the little brother that would be his closest companion until he left home, was one. There Wesley was a tenant farmer. [13]

Because at that time there were no colored schools in the Franklin area Buddy did not attend school until he was 11 when his family moved to the Wheelock community. There he completed the first grade. The following year he repeated the first grade in the Calvert Public Colored School. When the family moved again to the Beck Prairie Community he entered the second grade when he was 13. His mother's statement to the social worker indicated that he left school that year because he was slow to learn. His able minded siblings left school at the same grade level. In that setting going to work took priority over going to school. [14]

Cotton was labor intensive work that required the hands to be in the fields from February or March when the fields were cultivated for planting until the cotton was all picked and delivered to the gin by Thanksgiving. Through the spring, weeds had to be hoed away from the seedlings to assure that no foreign plant material would contaminate the cotton fibers at the gin. Later the maturing plants were thinned to a uniform spacing so as to maximize the water available to each maturing plant. All of this work required long days in the fields and it required skill.

With his father, Buddy's inability to keep a job may well have explained the beatings. There his "weak mind" limited his ability to stay on task, to perceive in sequence what was expected of him and to resists his impulsive urges to wander. A field hand who left patches of weeds or failed to thin the plants uniformly threatened the quality of the crop. Buddy's body was well built and dexterous but his work performance was poor and undependable. It was hard for his father and neighbors to understand why he never kept a job. In the vernacular of that time and place he was regarded as "just lazy and shiftless." Another neighbor wrote that during the time his parents worked for him he worked Buddy "two or three days at a time." [15]

Wesley was the son of former slaves. In the culture of slavery work and the significance of a man's life were synonymous. It was his burden, his enslavement, but if a human did not work he had no value. If a work animal did not work he was whipped. If a human did not work, he was whipped. In almost every letter to the Classification Officer Wesley and Lizzie were characterized as hardworking and that virtue justified a plea for clemency for their son. The other cold reality of that Depression Era was that sheer survival depended on every family member being able to work enough "to earn his bread."

That he was always looking for work followed him as his most notable characteristic. This never changed. What did change was the environment that surrounded him and the type of work available to him. All that Lizzie knew was that her son had left home looking for work. For two years before the bad tidings brought to her from the newspaper stories, the only thing she had known of him was the allotment check received from CCC. Often found beside her mailbox she awaited the letters he claimed to have written that she never received. She bragged to the mailman about her son in the Tree Army and with a mother's heart believed that he was working and doing well. The mail carrier took pleasure in the opportunity that his job gave him to read to her whatever letters she did receive. Others in the community took pleasure in receiving that news. Lorene Stephenson, the teacher, wrote that his little brothers danced with joy because now they were rich. [16]

When the news of the brutal attack in Clarendon reached Lizzie, her neighbors rallied around her in support. Mr. Stellbauer wrote letters to authorities inquiring about more details of the legal proceedings against Buddy. In advance of the letters of reference from the Bureau of Classification he joined with 24 citizens of Robertson County, bankers, businessmen, farmers, to petition the Board of Pardons and Parole for clemency in behalf of the weak minded boy they had known as Buddy. They responded promptly to the requests for the Bureau of Classification and waited hopefully for clemency. All that was known came from the press and those reports were conflicted. Reports from south Texas, still smarting from the abuses of an earlier and corrupted Texas Ranger force, made accusations of a coerced confession and false charges. Press in the Panhandle reinforced the image of "one of the most brutal attackers in Texas history." [17]

Early in December there was finally a letter for Mr. Stellbrauer to read to her. Written on a blank sheet of paper without letterhead and with only the number 208 written in the upper hand right margin it read:

"December 8th, 1938
Dear Mr. and Mrs. Norman,
Bremond, Texas

It becomes my sad duty to inform you that unless the Board of Pardons and Paroles, Austin, Texas, intervene, the death penalty assessed your son, Morris Norman, will be carried out in the early morning hours of December 16, 1938.

Please get in touch with me immediately and advise me what disposition you want made of the body, we must have advance information and will kindly ask you to have an undertaker get in touch with us now, if you wish to claim the body. If not, burial will take place in the Prison Cemetery with full Christian Rites. The State of Texas does not furnish a coffin except in case the burial is at the Prison Cemetery.

For your information I wish to state that everything possible is being done for your son to make his last few remaining hours as happy as possible.

Sincerely,
W. W. Waid, Warden
WWW/ce" [18]

On December 15, 1938 the *Donley County Leader* reported that the Board of Pardons and Paroles had concluded their investigation of extenuating circumstances and found none. The Board released the following report:

"He made a written confession fully detailing the horrible facts. We have a report from both the medical supervisor and the psychiatrist of the Texas prison system to the effect the subject is of sound mind and shows no evidence of psychosis or other mental abnormalities.

There is not a single mitigating fact or circumstance to be found in the entire record. The penalty assessed by the jury was well deserved and the subject should be executed at the time and place and in the manner stated by the sentence of the court." [19]

"You've been declared competent, son. Know what that means" Means you gonna ride the lightning." Green Mile [20]

No one can know the agony that surged through her mother's soul when she heard that news. Huntsville was 98 miles away, more distance than she had likely ever journeyed in her life, the cost of a funeral more money than she had ever known. A son was lost. But however heavy the burden of the grief she bore she bore it in the midst of community. Beck Prairie and the folks in Western Robertson County were just those kinds of neighbors. They worked together, played together, fought together, worshipped together and stuck together in times of adversity. [21]

And however unlikely it seems, Buddy would spend his last hours in community as well. Inmates in the prison tailor shop would take his measurements and fashion a suit, probably the first he ever wore. In the machine shop inmates would use metal stencils and black paint to chisel his name and epitaph into a rough cement tablet. In the carpentry shop they would fashion a simple wooden box for his coffin. Inmates with mattock and shovels who dug his grave would act as pallbearers and with the dirt of his grave still clinging to their hands and boots, remove their caps and serve as mourners. [22] It is said there are few flowers here.

"There is Balm in Gilead,
To make the wounded whole. . .
Come here, Jesus, come here, please." [23]

Loving, playful, innocent, Little Weena, grateful for the caring of The Time Traveler, remained at his side giving him flowers. She asked for nothing more. She perished in the flames he ignited to check the advancing cruelty of the Morlochs ... [24]

15

Little Weena's Flowers

O<small>N THE EVENING</small> before Morris Norman was to die for his crime against them, Cora and Mattie were informed by one of the Texas Rangers about the pending execution. "I wish I hadn't known the date. I wish we didn't know," they exclaimed. Sourced by the Ranger, the *Amarillo Globe News* article characterized the sisters as ""little old ladies in their modest home in the outskirts of Clarendon" and continued to describe the execution:

"Hundreds of miles away at Huntsville an electrical machine was being tuned.

A few moments after the midnight hour –when the modest home at Clarendon was dark -- the machine whined. A charge of legal electricity surged through the body of one of the most brutal attackers in Texas history, and he died.

Quoting a witness to Norman's brief visit with his family on his way to Huntsville, the article concluded:

"Boy," suggested an old negro mammy, "you better pray."

"He did last night just before he sat down in the state's electric chair." [1]

Justification for such an article was multiple. Firstly, it was sensationalism, the fuel that, as always, continues to keep the press going. But it was also propaganda. From the onset of the case, the agenda of the

Texas Ranger who allowed himself to be interviewed by the Amarillo paper had been to keep peace in the Panhandle. In an effort to assuage the lust of the mob, to uphold the cause of Southern honor for the virtue of womanhood, to justify the deterrent effects of the death penalty and bolster the merits of the updated state police force, he fed details to the press and it printed them. Lost in that maze of rhetoric was the human dignity of the victims, their attacker and his family. They were reduced to "little old ladies, an old negro mammy and a cold-blooded negro." [2]

On the night in 1938 when Orson Welles' "War of the Worlds" broadcast frightened millions with staged fantasies of ominous creatures wriggling out of the shadows in New Jersey, the drama whose plot was a war between worlds was upstaged by the eminence of war erupting within this planet and mocked by what happened beside a dump ground in Clarendon, Texas. At the vortex of the swirl of human lives caught up in what happened there was mankind at war with its own morality. The true prophesy within the broadcast was the reminder of H. G. Well's 1898 question: "What if cruelty had grown into a common passion?," [3] and the use of sound waves invading the airways to deliver the message.

Fear of aliens from Mars has waned by now. The expansion of the technology has advanced us to the point that the Rover jauntily crawled over the surface of Mars with little notice and NASA hopes to send men to that planet and we casually assume they will. The latest news is that there is water there. Unnoticed, the real menace has invaded us from within. "What if in this interval the race had lost its manliness, and had developed into something inhuman, unsympathetic, and overwhelmingly powerful?" [4] The aliens to be feared are not from outer space but those we have created within ourselves - neighbor alienated from neighbor, parents alienated from their own children, mankind from its humanity and societies from principal. The message is simple and it is terrifying. Alienation begets cruelty and cruelty begets cruelty.

Buddy's life was that cruelty. Through a chain of adversity, deprivation and abuse, he was robbed of the capacity to be fully human, sensitive and compassionate. His wanderings were aimless and detached as a piece of debris in the whirlwind, serving for little more than a reflection of that which swirled about him. At times his passions were powerful and ungovernable. At other times his only wish was a plaintiff childlike wish to see his mother one more time, to return to the nurturing of her pillow. In his wanderings through his Texas community he was forever seeking work. There he met congeniality with congeniality. In the streets of Chicago and beyond he learned the sordid and violent. Even there he performed well and was a dependable employee for a man who perhaps served as a positive father figure. [5] As he was committing a violent rape he remembered hearing the sounds of his victim's prayers.[6] With all of his cruelty he carried the seeds of nurturing that his mother had sown.

Society's view of him was as with a kaleidoscope, a different picture with every turn. On a dark night beside a dump ground a young black man with a prominent scar down the middle of his forehead committed a senseless act of violence upon two elderly white women. From the perspective of that community he was a brute who had violated two of its most respectable citizens without reason. His expressionless face was characterized as ebony black, smug and pretentious. No mention was made of the scar or his manner of speaking. His emotional responses were noted as apathetic toward his crime but nervous in the presence of authorities of the justice system. He was the source of outrage for his crime and a menace to the safety of the community.

The responsibility held by the Clarendon citizens for Buddy's inevitable fate was to assure that it was carried out by the legal system and not at the hands of a mob. That was not certain until he was safely delivered into the care of the Texas Prison System in Huntsville. Under the pressure of smoldering mob fury fueled by the rape of a white woman. Clarendon citizens took action and did it swiftly within the "code of honor" principles they held as a community.

In his home community he was known as the weak minded son of a hardworking but mean and overbearing tenant farmer and his very religious, humble and hardworking wife. His mother said he was well behaved and never required harsh discipline. He was the frail infant that she carried on a pillow. He was considered humble and obedient by most, never smiling, inept at working consistently but always wandering in search of work. Sometimes impetuous, he was called "Must Have It" by some of his peers. A neighborhood school teacher and the mail carrier remembered him as the victim of severe beatings from his father. No mention was made of the scar or his speech. His intelligence was rated as slow to learn because he had whooping cough as an infant. The responsibility felt by that community was to be good neighbor to their own. [7]

To his father, the mulatto son of a slave, he never had good sense and could not be depended to work and contribute to the family. [8] It is not certain at what point a white man entered his ancestry or what level of cruelty that represented, but within the culture of slaves and slave owners, a black man was a work animal who had no value if he did not work. Extending far beyond slavery within a segment of the agrarian society was the belief that beating a work animal to produce work was no more cruel than it is for a modern farmer to put fuel into the gas tank of his tractor.

To Mose Dean, the black neighbor who took Buddy into his home to spare him the beatings, he was trustworthy. In his semi-literate writing Mose described Buddy, "To say to you the truth, Norman not so bright in sense. His most habit is eating and eating plenty. Never seemed to care for girl company somehow. That why I no he is trusty around familys." Mose concluded his letter with a benediction for us all. "Truth demonstrated is eternal life. God, infinite, all power, all life, truth, love, over all and all." To the mother of Mose and likely "the old negro mammy," he was the victim of the beatings from his father who was extended a sanctuary within her family. There he received food, "and plenty of it" at their table and Christian teachings from the religious fervor within that home. [9]

To a volunteer worker for the Chicago Travel Aids Society he was a stranded transient who had wandered in off of the cold streets of Chicago. She noted his Negroid features and the noticeable scar running lengthwise on his forehead. She also noted his slow, stuttering speech and the vagueness of its content. She recorded his social history as that of an elder son of a large, impoverished tenant farm family from Texas and the level of his education as second grade completed when he was thirteen. [10]

In the descriptions he gave of himself to social workers and criminal investigators, he had performed in the Eastern Star Rodeo, worked as an attendant for a barn storming pilot on runs between Texas and Chicago, served as an errand boy for a furniture store and a procurer, the legal term, or pimp in the street world, for a house of prostitution at 46th and Calumet in Chicago. [11]

At the Texas Prison System his identification was Texas Ex 208, a product to be duly processed under the Death Row standards of that time and executed on December 16th.[12] We have to remember the words of the executioner in The Green Mile, "What am I gonna say? That it was my job? My job?" [13] And that it was we, the people, who wrote the job description.

The 1936 Legislature created the Bureau of Classification whose job it was to interview the incoming inmate to create a "social summary" that included criminal history, the prisoner's version of the crime, family history, mental status and general summary of the prisoner.[14] This Classification Summary described him as a tall, well-built individual with ebony-black skin, stolid features and undemonstrative expression. The scar on his forehead was included in the Texas Prison System's Description of the Convict When Received form. On the line marked "Marks, Scars and General Remarks" it read: "vertcct sc mid 4hd." Also included on that line were abbreviated descriptions of scars on his hand, a curved scar at the base of the front of his neck and a Smallpox vaccination. His social history was given as one who was unstable with poor adaptation to his home environment and ability to accept and hold steady employment. His emotional responses were described as nervous but co-operative. Comments about his mental status were that he had difficulty in remembering and spelling names, used rationalization to describe his history, had no gross personality defects and had the language and mannerisms of the average tenant farm negro.[15]

The Medical Supervisor for the Texas Prison System reported to the Board of Pardons and Paroles that he did not see any evidence of any mental abnormality just that he seemed to be an average Negro. The findings of the four page psychiatric examination of Morris Norman by the consulting psychiatrist for the prison was summarized "the subject was of sound mind with no evidence of psychosis or other mental abnormalities."[16] The case of Morris Norman added evidence to support a theory about genetic inferiority.

Based on the facts presented to them the three-member Board of Pardons and Parole found that Morris Norman was of sound and normal mind. They concluded that he had confessed to a horrible crime, rape of a white woman, and that he had deliberately planned and executed it. No mitigating factors were noted by this board.

To the society of the Southland In 1938, Southerners still clinging to the idealistic notions of chivalry and the sanctity of womanhood, he represented the stereotype of the lustful black man. The rape of a white woman, especially by a black man, was unforgivable and the consensus of public opinion required that it be punished by death, at the hands of zealots for this "peculiar chivalry" or by the law. Lynchings were still all too common and they were often barbaric. One of the first actions in Texas designed to stop them was the 1922 capital punishment legislation providing a legal means at the state level for execution, with rape as a capital offense. The majority of rape trials concluded with that verdict. Legal appeal was maintained as a right but not as a mandate. The clemency process, streamlined in 1936 under Governor Allred, enhanced this last option to the convicted rapist [17] though since 1922 it was not until 1960 that the first black convicted of rape was not executed because of an intervention by the Board of Pardons and Parole.[18]

What he was to his victims is largely unknown. One press interview of the rape victim described her as outraged and quoted her plea for justice by means of the law. The transcript of the trial was "misfiled" in the court house records. On the eve of the execution both victims told a reporter that they wished they had not known about the date of the execution.[19] The story of the tragedy was quickly forgotten by all but the immediate friends and families of the victims. Some recalled that they remained reclusive and shy only venturing out to attend church. No one spoke of the route they took after the crime or their means of travel. Society's concept of support for them was never speaking of it again. No doubt the hideous wounds wrought by the tragedy remained heavy, painful and erosive in their hearts for the rest of their lives, but because what had happened to them was a secret mandated by the "peculiar chivalry" code they became hidden, nonpersons, largely sealed away from historic retrospection. The accomplishments and qualities of these lives remained buried like the treasures in King Tutt's tomb until this search made it possible to partially bring them to life.

For 46 days two communities of concerned citizens, a newly formed network of law enforcement officers, an updated Board of Pardons and Parole and a seasoned execution system grappled with case of Morris Norman. In the end there was no clemency. At 12:05 a.m., December 16, 1938, Morris Norman died in the electric chair. He was the 208th person to be sentenced to death by electrocution and the last person executed during the term of Governor Jimmy Allred. W. Lee O'Daniel, elected on the day he was sentenced to die, was inaugurated as Governor of Texas. He opposed he death penalty.[20] Donley County was billed $25.00 for the execution and $8.95 for his burial suit.[21] The local press announced the execution as a victory for justice and dropped the matter as a sign-off to the story.

Buddy's story was not an historic "sign off" but a standard by which the then and now for the evolution of our legal system and our social and moral principles can be evaluated. In 1938 a cold wind was sweeping through the universe over decaying pockets of humanity. In the Southland white supremacy and male dominance cloaked itself in a "peculiar chivalry." The need to cull out the unfit in an agrarian culture denoted an evitable fate for an egg sucking dog or a glass eyed horse. A school of pseudoscience championed genetic cleansing and in Eastern Europe an Arian group took up the cause. In Huntsville, Texas, a black rapist had but one destiny.

". . . you gonna ride the lightening. . . " [22]

"Evolving standards of decency" has been stated by some jurists as a goal for legislative processes by the Supreme Court in the evolution of Eighth and Fifth Amendment findings. Over the ages the social response to those with less than normal mental capacity has ridden a wide swinging pendulum from the time in Ancient France and Rome when they were declared to be just barely human incapable of deliberate intent to harm to the Western society of the 20's that believed them to be innately moral degenerates. Within our present moral conscience the pendulum is still swinging. [23]

Throughout time words used to name the condition have also run the euphemistic treadmill. Terms now thought to be stigmatizing or derogatory were once scientific terms used in attempts to better describe or even to euphonize it. Some examples are idiot, moron, imbecile, feeble-minded, developmental delay. Rhetoric included in *Ex Parte Tuttle* presented to the Court of Criminal Appeals of Texas on July 9, 1969, for a murder committed April 23, 1938, used terms such as "low grade intellect of a moronic type," "insanity of a criminal type," "so feeble-minded as to be legally insane." Only recently the official medical term mental retardation has been changed to intellectual disability. [24]

The dilemma was well defined by the work of psychiatrist Dr. Lewis:

"We, as a society of thinking and feeling human beings, struggle within ourselves to cope with competing interests and motivations: the need for protection from dangerous people, sane or insane; the desire for revenge; the knowledge of psychobiological and environmental influences upon violent behavior; and the wish to adapt to evolving standards of decency and morality. Guilt was a lot easier to measure before we recognized that free will, like sanity and insanity, is a constantly fluctuating intellectual and emotional continuum and not a fixed, immutable capacity or state of mind." [25]

He stood at the edge of life's highway, at the edge of logic - lost, homeless, expressionless, without significance - somewhere between the humble negro boy and the cold-blooded rapist. In his fantasies he subdued bucking broncs before cheering rodeo crowds. He soared through the skies aboard his private plane. He was gigantic and powerful. He walked the final thoroughfare, the green mile, with flash and front. His suit was spun-gold shot through with precious stones. His shoes were dazzling silver.

"But does he deserve death?" Her question still sounds in our conscience. In 1938 he was declared death eligible by a Donley County jury, a Houston psychiatrist for the Texas prison system, the Board of Pardons and Paroles and by the public opinion of that time. Even after the 2002 *Virginia v. Atkins* Supreme Court decision to abolish execution of those with mental impairments, a convoluted system for defining those impairments or permitting the definition to be admitted into evidence still confuse the issue. The matter of death eligibility for those with mental impairments, traumatic brain injuries, childhood abuse and deprivation continues to be largely unresolved. But as long as the question remains in debate it is at least in the conscience of man and in that there is hope.

Still bound to the moral "code of honor" to protect the sanctity of womanhood in 1938 the citizens of Donley County and its legal system acted swiftly on this principle to sentence to death a self-confessed rapist. The status of his mental state was not a consideration. There was little understanding of the condition and few accepted legal standards in place to deal with it. If Buddy were tried today on a capital offense, whatever the intent of *Virginia v. Atkins*, the interpretations of his mental state within our current legal procedures still leaves the possibility that he would be found death-eligible. Conversely, society's regard for the sanctity of womanhood or for sexual morality itself has been degraded to a level that shames us. Seventy-five years later in the same courtroom where Buddy was sentenced to death, a man confessed to multiple rapes of a seven year old girl and walked away with no more than a ten year term of probation. [26] Man without his humanity?

The Time Traveler returned from his journey into the future with grave concerns about man's cruelty and the demise of his humanity. But he also brought back his story of little Weena, creature of that far distant time zone when man's humanity was but a memory. He had seen the little thing drowning before the very eyes of her fellow creatures. Not one of them made the slightest attempt to save her – the gravest cruelty, not caring. He rescued her from drowning and restored life to her little body. What followed during his brief stay in that time zone was a shower of gratitude and tenderness from her bestowed upon him in the form of simple white flowers stuffed into his pockets. Tragically, she perished in the fire that the Time Traveler ignited with matches found in his pocket to initiate his efforts to stay the cruelty of the Mordocks of the underworld. He returned to the present with both some of the matches and little Weena's flowers still in his pockets. [27]

Late in the writing of the final chapter to this story an email with an attached historical newspaper article was received as an addendum to research queries submitted much earlier. It was as though the voice of Orson Welles was saying, "We interrupt the writing of this story to bring to your attention a heretofore unknown news story written by a Houston Post reporter who witnessed the execution of Morris Norman. Representing the last statement issued by Norman, the article read:

"Huntsville Dec 16 – Morris Norman, 20-year old Clarendon negro went to his death in a execution early Friday – but he went down as the first man in the prison history to dress for the electric chair with spats on his feet.

Norman, condemned of criminal assault on a middle-age Clarendon woman in 1938, walked to the chair with a pair of pearl-gray spats buttoned nattily above his prison brogans.

The other items of his attire – a prison made shirt and blue suit contrasted sharply with the dandified ankle gear.

The negro made no final statement before taking his seat in the chair. He claimed from the beginning that he was under the effects of a cigarette filled with aspirin before the assault on the white woman, a spinster, was made." [28]

The Time Traveler vanished into the unchartered abyss of time having spoken to his friends with despair about the ultimate outcome - what if cruelty had grown into a common passion and mankind had lost its humanity? Buddy's life becomes a metaphor for mankind without its manliness, man without his capacity to reason, overwhelmed by his own power, wandering aimlessly in search of significance in a world that denied him significance. In the end Buddy's significance was marked by the brief time his family was rich because of his allotment check and he was the first man in Texas history to walk the green mile wearing spats. "My shoes would be dazzling silver." [29] Dressed in the prison tailored shirt and blue suit, "dandified" by a pair of pearl-gray spats nattily buttoned above his prison brogans, he walked to the chair explaining the loss of his sensibility to himself with the fantasy of an "asparine cigarette". With no other statement, he took his seat in man's response to his cruelty. Lived out at the dump ground of our social conscience Buddy's life represented the alpha and omega of cruelty.

"Never said a mumbalin' word.
Lightenin' flashes, thunders roll,
Make me think of my poor soul,
Come here, Jesus, come here please." [30]

In closing his story H.G. Wells' Time Traveler left behind the remains of two white flowers – the Fourth Dimension, that which endured. The flowers were reminders of a moment in which he had exchanged tenderness with Little Weena, leaving us with the plaintiff hope that as long as the capacity for gratitude and mutual tenderness remains in the heart of mankind it will not perish. Mankind, recreated with every birthing, is a new creature designed to become the endowment of belonging, loving and creativity or to be redesigned for the want of it.

The hope is spoken when a teacher, a mail carrier, or a banker reaches out with kindness to a child standing expressionless beside the highway of life. When a child sees the look of duty in her father's face as his head is bowed in prayer over a newspaper and she wonders why, she may one day stand in the crimson Poppy fields of France where he served and notice that all of the crosses are equal. There a soldier can stand in a moment of prayer over the grave of a vanquished foe out of reverence both for the life he had taken and the cause for which he had waged the war. In a later time she may stand upon Peckerwood Hill and look down upon a jumbled assembly of crude cement crosses and tablets and contemplate this expression of man's intolerance for cruelty. From wherever white flowers unstained by man's cruelty still bloom, she may bring two white flowers and with little Weena's hope for mankind, lay them at Buddy's feet. In that far shady corner where he rests, his epitaph, the number 208, she can anticipate a time when man's intolerance for cruelty may be tempered by his intolerance for its causes. And in remembering with reverence all the diverse elements of humanity that swirled within Buddy's story, feel content that the answer to her father's prayer was in the telling of the story, and for his caring, dedicate a flower from Little Weena.

16

Epilogue

No RAPE VICTIM ever erases the searing jagged scar to self and soul. They live beyond it. The wounds of some continue to bleed; some like oysters surround their wounds with pearls, but deep within the wound remains. Whatever happened with Cora and Mattie Lee was shrouded in secrecy. They retreated into obscurity. Their friends and family members chose to keep the details of their lives secret in order to protect and respect them. Sadly, the real tragedy of secrets is that the very acts of guarding such secrets actually generate the psychological suffering of the victims and avoiding any reality of the trauma only fortifies the extent of the fear and pain it causes.[1]

Forty years after the attack at the dump ground attorney John Knorpp, one of Morris Norman's defense lawyers, remembered that it had been one of the swiftest trials in the history of Texas but did not recall details of the crime and certainly not the victims. [2]

Seventy-five years later a search through citizens who lived in Clarendon in 1938 yielded only one who recalled anything about the crime. A fellow church member who as a young bride bought fresh milk from the Ferris sisters sighed and said: "They never got over what happened to them." She declined to give details. [3]

One man who attended church with Cora Ferris in the 1970's remembered her as the vibrant singer who wore her silver white hair pulled away from her face into a bun and quoted poetry to the congregation. She never missed a service and this man, not knowing the significance of it, said she walked to church. Even today the only viable route to her home would lead her past the site of the old dump ground. [4]

History records Mattie Lee Jones and Cora Ferris as:

"little old ladies in their modest home in the outskirts of Clarendon," the "two Donley County women who were raped on their way home from church." [5]

Piercing the shrouds of secrecy that surround the life story of Cora Ferris has been difficult to research. At no point in her life would anyone who knew her have described her as just a little old lady, Her ancestors were well known pioneers, the site of her birth historically picturesque and her career as school teacher adventuresome.

Navajoe, Oklahoma Territory, the site of her birth, was a typical frontier town of more than 200 families. It had its share of gunfights and historical outlaw activity. It also had its share of frontier hardships and tragedy. It flourished for more than 15 years until the coming of the railroad. Overnight the dwellings of the village were loaded onto wagons and hauled to the rails that had located seven miles away. All that remains of Navajoe today is a picturesque cemetery at the foot of the mountains. Marked there are things seen of the winds that passed through Cora Ferris' family

James Monroe Ferris and his wife, Martha Jane Stanford Ferris, left Tarrant County, Texas in 1887 with their family of six surviving children to join the first families to inhabit Navajoe. Mattie Lee, their second child, was 12. Cora, their tenth child, would join the family six years later.

U. S. Deputy Marshal James (Jim) M. and wife Martha J. Ferris came to Navajoe in 1887. They had eleven children.

James was a frontier lawman throughout his adult life, U. S Secret Service, U.S Marshall, Texas Ranger and Deputy Sheriff. What his children remembered about his work as a lawman were his long unannounced absences from which he returned silent and grim faced, never speaking to his family about the things he had experienced. When Cora was two and Mattie twenty, the family remembers watching their father racing his horse to the house, dismounting to hurriedly wrap a silk scarf around a bleeding wound to his leg, remounting and galloping off to continue his mission. In retrospect the family surmised that he had joined in the area manhunt for the Rufus Buck Gang in the summer of 1895.

The Buck Gang, made up of a Creek Mulatto, Buck, and four others who were Creeks and Creek Blacks, had been the target of a territory wide sweep by lawmen after they went on a thirteen day rampage of robberies, murders and savage gang rapes of women of all these races. After their capture the lawmen held back the lynch mobs made up of the members' own people until the gang members could stand trial and sentencing in a court of law. His daughters never heard about these things from him. He had put his life at risk to assure the safety of the citizens of his Territory. Half a century later his daughters would become victims of a crime of almost equal savagery.

The children's fonder memories of their father were as an orchard and livestock farmer. People from all over the Navajoe area came to buy fruit from the large orchard that graced his land. From a very young age he schooled his children in farming and livestock management by designating a tree in the orchard for them and giving each one of them a calf, a colt and a pig to do with as they pleased. He told them that "if they were wise they would make money." Mattie followed this model of livelihood her entire life. Living on her orchard and vegetable farm she maintained her livestock and milk cows until her death at 88. In her years as a retired school teacher Cora joined her sister in the operation of the farm and remained there until her last years.

What the children remembered of Martha Jane, their mother, was her devotion to the Navajo church. She enthusiastically promoted the summer revivals and no doubt joined the temperance movement that removed the saloons from Navajoe. One of the few supporting documents of Cora's life was her Certificate of Baptism from the Navajoe church when she was four. It was a baptism in the crimson waters of the North Fork of Red River that flowed at the feet of the mountains.

The Ferris sisters would follow that model of devotion to the church established by their mother. Seventy-five years after the fateful night at the dump ground few if any people in Clarendon remembered Mattie Jones or Cora Ferris or details of what happened to them there. What is remembered is that they were two ladies on their way home from the church that spoke in tongues. The founding history of that denomination encompassed in the life of Cora Ferris left unnoted.

Things began to change in the Ferris family in 1898 when Mattie left the home. She met and married Greer County school teacher, Thomas E, Jones, and moved with him to the nearby village of Martha. The following spring as the east sun rose over the mountains and shimmered upon the delicate blossoms in the Ferris orchard Martha Jane gave birth to her 12th child, Aaron Monroe. Twelve days later death took her away. Sometime that same year Mattie gave birth to Thomas E. Jones, Jr. and laid him to rest in the Navajoe Cemetery in the shadows of her mother's grave. As Navajoe was being hauled away, Mattie moved with her husband to Clarendon in 1901. In 1908 Mattie laid a second child named Cora in the Navajoe Cemetery beside her brother. One mile south of the cemetery the Ferris farm remained in the family name for generations to come. [6]

Though it was known that she had taught in Oklahoma, Texas, Louisiana and Mississippi and that she had completed 3 years of college no supporting documentation for any of this was found until the "time machine" located her at 501 Maple St., Biloxi, Mississippi in 1922. Beginning in 1919 an evangelical movement in the church devoted to the salvation of souls and witness through speaking in tongues had swept through Alabama, Mississippi and eastern Louisiana. In 1922 Rev. J.L. Slay pitched a large tent at the corner of Division and Lee in Biloxi and began a several week revival that concluded with the baptism of some 80 converts in the river at the edge of the property. On August 22, 1922 the Central Assembly of God Church was formed with 71 charter members. Cora's residence was three-quarters of a mile from Division and Lee.

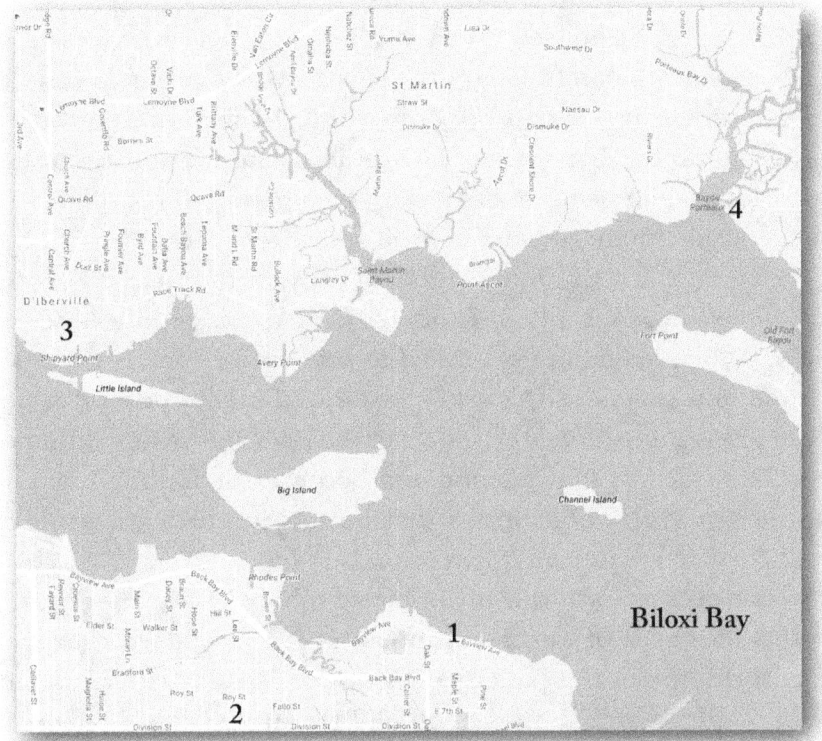

Known to be in Biloxi, Mississippi during the 1922-23 school year, Cora Ferris lived at the end of Maple Street (1); three-quarters of a mile from the Assembly of God Church at the corner of Division and Lee Streets (2); taught at the County Line School near D'Iberville (3). Brother Isaiah's colony lived in house boats near Bayou Porteaux (4).

Cora was Assistant Principle in a school across the bay that consolidated several small schools in the remote and isolated sections of southwestern Jackson County with a more accessible site in eastern Harrison County near the ferry landing and town of D'Iberville. It was fondly known as "the little green school:"

In June of 1922 another historic religious movement in the person of Brother Isaiah moved into the north shore of the Back Bay at the eastern edge of the Harrison-Jackson County Line school district near St.

Martin. Arriving from New Orleans in his "fleet" of seven vessels, boats and houseboats, he and his twenty-five followers set up tents along the shore and tilled the land for food. He and the men of his group wore long hair and grew heavy beards. Brother Isaiah was distinguished by his very long white beard and shock of grey hair. Women of the group wore no facial enhancement and lived apart from the men.

The ferry that Cora took to school crossed the Back Bay within 2 miles of the shoreline where Brother Isaiah's community of tents was located. While his followers worked to provide for him, Brother Isaiah preached and practiced the art of healing. Daily hundreds of people flocked to his camp along the shores of the Back Bay to hear him preach and to be healed of their mental and bodily afflictions. Some said he performed miracles and others that he was just a deluded old man. Nonetheless he created an impression.

As picturesque as "the little green school" were the families it served. This area of west Jackson County was isolated from the rest of the world due to the paucity of good roads and sufficient bridges. This allowed the indigenous people of the area occupying the north shore of the Back Bay of Biloxi from Biglin Bayou in Harrison County on the west, to the mouth of Fort Bayou on the east, to maintain the French language and Roman Catholic religion of their ancestors for many generations. It was common to hear a dialect of French spoken by the people here into the 1950's. Their English was accented which identified their place of origin. To the natives of Biloxi anyone from North Biloxi, as it was known to almost everyone on the south shore, was "a hoss from across." [7]

Cora's next school was in the Cormardelle Village School in the heart of Cajun country. This school was a short boardwalk away from the newly organized Assembly of God Church located in the Sanctified Church. [8]

For the 34 years of their marriage, Mattie Lee Jones spent her life at the side of her husband, Thomas E. Jones, first, as the quiet man-nered school teacher from Kansas and later as a prominent orchard and garden farm producer. After his death she remained on their farm and carried on that work until her death in 1964. [9]

▲ ▲ ▲

Members of the justice system that brought Morris Norman to trial and conducted the trial were quickly dispersed by World War II. Sheriff Guy Pierce re-enlisted in the Army and served as a Special Investigator. After the war he located in the San Antonio area where he was involved in the lumber business. His wife, Mary, was involved in that family business and later became a real estate broker.[10]

District Attorney, John Deaver, re-enlisted in the Marine Corps where he served as an officer in the Judge Advocate Branch until several years after the war. He returned to his law practice in Memphis until his death in 1978.

In providing a photograph of his uncle for this writing, John M. Deaver, II, reviewed the 1938 newspaper clipping of the trial and made the following comment:

"I was appalled at the characterization in the articles as a hell bent for leather aggressive prosecutor bowing to the pressures of the prejudices expressed by the author of the newspaper articles. My guess is, attempting to imagine the mood of the times, that there was no real doubt of a conviction being had, and that this wise prosecutor sought to conclude the trial as quickly as possible, and have the defendant removed from the volatile crowd that was likely to have been demanding its version of *justice*."[11]

Texas Ranger, Neal Arthur, resigned from the Rangers in 1942 and enlisted in the Army as Special Investigator. After the war he worked as a Private Investigator and retired as a General Claims Agent for the Southern Pacific Railroad. [12]

Texas Ranger, Pat Taliaferro, was discharged from the Rangers in 1941. He also served in the Army and returned to the Amarillo area after the war. In 1945 he pleaded guilty to a driving while intoxicated charge, second offense, and was given a five year suspended sentence. He spent his last days in Bisbee, Arizona. [13]

John Knorpp, defense attorney, served in the Army and returned to Clarendon to practice law and carry on his family insurance business. [14]

From 1942 to 1945 Dr. Abe Hauser served as a lieutenant colonel in the United States Air Corps as a flight surgeon. He returned to Houston to serve as clinical professor in the Department of Neurology at Baylor Medical School, Houston (1949-1974), and professor of neurology and psychiatry emeritus at UTMB, Galveston, from 1974. He passed away June 2, 1991. [15]

Judge A. S. Moss finished his last term as 100th District Judge in 1944 and retired to Tulia, Texas.[16]

A heart attack took the life of defense attorney, Judge Ralph Porter, in October of 1956. [17]

Mr. C. L. Goin, foreman of the jury, died in his home in July of 1956. "His activities had been limited after being struck by lightening a few years ago." [18]

Judge Link and Mr. Green died of natural causes in the 1960's. [19]

R. Y. King retired from the practice of law in 1956. After his wife died of a sudden stroke in 1957 he spent some time in New Mexico with his sister and finally came to live with his daughter, Ruth Ann, and her husband, attorney Broadus Spivey. Spivey recalled that Mr. King spent many an hour telling him stories about the many cases he remembered during his law career. Spivey commented that he never mentioned the case of Morris Norman. [20]

▲ ▲ ▲

The matter of Buddy entered the same tomb of secrecy in Robertson County as it had in Clarendon. Seventy-five years hence no one recalled it or if they did, declined to discuss it. If there were prayers over the newspapers in Robertson County that day, they are to be seen only in terms of Mose Dean's words, "I must say truth demonstrated is eternal life."

On New Year's Eve the following year, 1939, Lorene Stephenson, the teacher, was married in her church following the Sunday evening preaching service. Her groom, Carl Foster, was from the Boons community near the Petteway School where she was teaching. He worked as a machinist for the Hughes Tool Company during the time that the flamboyant Howard Hughes, Jr. had ventured into the airline business and, in co-operations with Brown Shipbuilding Co., initiated one of America's most thriving defense contracting industries along the Houston Ship Channel. After a brief honeymoon trip he returned to his job in Houston and she stayed on in the home of her parents until she finished that school year.

In the summer of 1940 Lorene joined her husband at 2508 Spence in Houston where she would spend the next 58 years of her life. In 1942 she brought her younger brother, Weldon, the little brother whose toys she shared with Buddy and his little brother, into her home. He was among the first to join the work force at the nearly formed Brown Shipbuilding Company. He was eighteen and his new job was as an electrician. By May of 1943 the Brown Shipbuilding Company was turning out destroyer escorts at the rate of one per week. The future looked bright for Carl, the machinist, and for Weldon, the budding young electrician.

The news of the tragedy that rocked the lives of Lorene and her family did not come from foreign battle fields; it came to her from down the street. At 12:15 p.m. on August 4, 1943, Weldon died in an industrial accident at Brown Shipbuilding Company. He was electrocuted.

They brought him home to the community of his childhood and laid him to rest in the peaceful Nesbitt Cemetery. There the tall pillar-like tombstone his family placed at his grave stood as a centennial overlooking the cemetery and family plots awaiting his childhood neighbors and the open green turf in nearby Rose Hill Cemetery awaiting his black neighbors. One by one, over the years, they have joined him there.

Lorene's thirty-five year career as a teacher in the De Chaumes Elementary School brought her to the front lines of the changes in the American school. She left the one room school house in the tranquil rural community of Petteway and began teaching in the large three story brick school building only a short distance from busy downtown Houston. By then schools were available to colored children though they were still segregated. Because of the rapid wartime migration of many other racial and ethnic children of color into the Houston schools, the matter of segregation was confusing. There were many special needs to be addressed. No doubt Lorene's "hope to help" spirit livened her teaching in this environment.

When she left this life on December 13, 1998, it was mentioned in her obituary that she taught school for 35 years in the De Chaume Elementary in HISD No one there today remembers Lorene Foster. The letter she wrote to Austin seventy- seven years ago remains archived in the State Library. It has had few readers. Nonetheless, she has left us her question and her hope. [21]

▲ ▲ ▲

The road ahead for Lizzie was a long one. For a decade she remained with her family in the Beck Prairie community. Walter stayed in the home and helped his ailing father with the farm work. In 1946 Wesley died of natural causes, unattended by a doctor. Adjacent to the Nesbitt-Beck Prairie Cemetery, he was laid to rest in the Rose Hill Memorial African American Cemetery. Lizzie moved to Calvert and spent the rest of *her* days close to her oldest daughter, Almery.

There would be more tragic funerals for Lizzie. Another son lay on a pillow of suffering in her care. For two years Harry received treatment for renal cancer and lived in her home. At age 31 he joined his father at Rose Hill. Four years later Lizzie received word that two of her son Fletcher's children, 7 and 9, had died of smoke inhalation when their tenant house burned in the night. An electrical short started the fire. A decade after that Fletcher drowned while trying to swim his horse across a swollen creek near Marlin.

For yet another decade Lizzie lived on. Plagued with illnesses of old age she survived in community with her church and neighbors. At the time of Fletcher's death she sold a life estate in her house and all of her belongings to a neighbor so that she could stay on there. A few days short of her 96th birthday she laid her burden down.

> *Quiet-like some still day, I'm just goin' home, ...*
> *Work all done, cares laid by, . . .I'm just goin' home."* [22]

Beneath a turf covered opening in the woods surrounding Rose Hill and Nesbitt Cemeteries, Lizzie rests with her husband and two youngest sons in an unmarked grave at the foot of native trees. In the far corner of the Rose Hill Cemetery, a cluster of tombstones mark the graves of the neighbor that sheltered her son before he roamed away and who stood by her for the brief time that he returned to her. Mose Dean, his wife, his father, the daughters he trusted with Buddy and his mother, probably "the old negro mammy" that admonished Buddy to pray for his salvation as he left for Huntsville. [23]

Rose Hill Cemetery in the foreground; Nesbitt Cemetery in the background.

Just as no man is an island, no crime occurs in isolation. Sucked into its vortex are the lives of its victims, its perpetrators, their families, the communities they represent, those responsible for justice systems involved in its resolution. Such a story rests within each of the hundreds of Death Row Inmate Files safely secured in the State Archives. As part of the mainland each of us are diminished by the debris left in its wake, and as a sober reminder, each of us are a part of the atmosphere that created the swirl.

A special tribute to the historic photography of
Ernest L. Hunt (1896 – 1959), and for the prayer
that inspired the telling of this story.

NOTES

Chapter 1
The Buttercup Years

1.) H. G. Wells, *The Time Machine* (The Random House Publishing Group, 1968), 9-93.

2.) "Services Held for Ham McCampbell," *The Donley County Leader,* October 2, 1966.

3.) Louva Hunt, *Jaypap,* unpublished manuscript.

4.) Author's note: Stationed along the sidewalks of Kearney Street, referred to by natives as Main Street, were wooden benches for the convenience of those who came to town to visit, not to shop. Since the majority of those seated there were elderly men many of whom chewed tobacco and some of whom aimlessly whittled on a wooden stick with a pocket knife, they were affectionately referred to as the Spit and Whittle Club.

5.) "KGNC: The Globe-News Radio Station," *Amarillo Sunday Globe-News,* October 30, 1938.

6.) John H. Lovell, e-mail message to Louva Hunt, May 13, 2015: "The box magazine on the side of the rifle is clicked open and 5 brass cartridges are dropped into the open magazine. With that done the magazine is snapped shut and the gun is ready to be fired by pushing a cartridge into the chamber with the bolt action and squeezing the trigger. The Krag was invented by the Norwegian, Ole Krag, and developed in collaboration with Erik Jorgenson. By the beginning of WWI it was 'obsolete' and the US Army was removing them from its arsenal." Author's note: At the time of his departure from Brest,

France in 1919, Ernest Hunt had the chance to accept the gun as a gift from the US Army and was allowed to bring it home with him. It was one of his most prized possessions.

7.) Benjamin Keck, "October 30 Memorable Night in '38," *Amarillo Daily News,* October 30, 1978.

8.) "Rulers of the Home to Present Their Royal Tom Thumb Wedding," *The Donley County Leader,* November 3, 1938.

9.) "Negro Charged With Assault Will Come To Trial Tues.," *The Donley County Leader,* November 3, 1938; "Rulers of the Home."

10.) "Justice Acts Speediest As Attacker Dies," *The Amarillo Globe,* December 16, 1938.

Chapter 2
The Time Machine

1. "Memorable Night."

2. *A scan of headlines in Amarillo Daily News, October 30, 1978.*

3. *The Holy Bible, Revised Standard Version,* Ecclesiastes I: 9.

4. H. G. Wells, 14.

5. "Memorable Night."

6. "Negro Charged With Assault Will Come to Trial Tues."

7. "Royal Tom Thumb Wedding."

8. Ann Hommel, letter to Louva Hunt, February 2, 1979.

9. H. G. Wells, 19.

10. "A Million Imaginations Afire As Radio Realism Shakes The Nation," *Amarillo Daily News, Octob*er 31, 1938.

11. "Donley County Grand Jury is Called in Attack Case," *Amarillo Daily News*, November 1, 1938.

12. H. G. Wells, *21-29.*

13. James W. Marquart, Sheldon Ekland-Olson, Jonathan R. Sorenson, *The Rope, the Chair, & the Needle: Capital Punishment in Texas, 1923-1990 (University of Texas Press, 1994), 52.*

14. "Negro Charged *With Assault Will Come to Trial Tues."*

15. "Justice Acts Speediest As Attacker Dies."

Chapter 3
The Settting

1.) "Memphis, Texas," *The Handbook of Texas Online: Texas State Historical Association;* tshaonline.org.

2.) Robert M. Utley, *Lone Star Lawman: The Second Century of Texas Rangers,* (Oxford University Press, 2007), 87.

3.) "Thousand Witness Parade of the Ku Klux Klan in Clarendon Last Thursday Evening," *The Clarendon News,* June 15, 1922.

4.) "To The Lovers of Law and Order," *The Clarendon News*, August 3, 1922.

5.) Sara R. Massey, ed., *Black Cowboys of Texas,* (Texas A&M Press, 2000), 226, 235.

6.) *Ibid.*, 216.

7.) "Bones Hooks . . . famous black cowboy and civic leader," Email Museum 1-5; pan-tex.net.

8.) Utley, 87.

9.) Broadus and Ruth Ann Spivey, interview with Louva Hunt, October 2, 2013.

10.) John Deaver, II, interview with Louva Hunt, February 20, 2013.

11.) Utley, 87.

12.) Clarendon Lore. The father of the author often advised, "It takes two to gossip, one to tell and one to listen, If one does not do both, then it isn't gossip." In Clarendon, as with many small towns, gossip has been known to attain the level of a Gladiator sport. The author hopes that by citing anonymously as Clarendon Lore things commonly heard throughout her lifetime will exempt it as being gossip.

13.) Utley, 176, 127.

14.) Willard Skelton, "A Little Bit of History." Christmas 2004.

15.) Clarendon Lore.

16.) History of *1930* Texas Lynchings: Utley, *Lone Star Lawmen*, 133-139, 140, 133-4, 140, 166, 190-1.

17.) *Ibid.*

18.) "Veteran Officer Added to Highway Patrol Forces Here," *Amarillo Globe*, September 29, 1938.

19.) *Ibid.*

20.) Tom Burk, interview with Louva Hunt, September, 2013.

21.) Vivian Allen interview with Louva Hunt, November 9, 2012.

22.) "Youth Confesses Robbery of Bank," *San Antonio Light, November 12, 1936.*

23.) "Plainview Murder Suspect Slain: Shot Down in Lockney Barn," *Abilene Reporte*r News, May 31, 1939.

24.) "Veteran Officer Added to Highway Forces Here."

Chapter 4
Appointment in Clarendon

1.) Ray Lunk, *Des Allemandes: A Bayou Runs Through It.* Lulu Enterprises, Inc., Raleigh, NC. 2011; 1930 United States Federal Census – Ancestry.com.

2.) "Navajoe, Texas – Navajoe, Okla. 100 Years Old -1887-1987," Museum of the Western Plains, Altus, Oklahoma.

3.) "Obituaries: Pierce," *The Clarendon Enterprise,* October 26, 2000.

4.) Cindy Barnett, e-mail message to Louva Hunt, August 6, 2012.

5.) "Timeless Tales: Jailer's Wife Shoots Escaping Prisoner," *Amarillo Globe-News, September 30, 1999;* "Woman Jailer Plays Big Part In Negro Hunt," *The Donley County Leader, November 3, 1938.*

6.) Clarendon Lore.

7.) "St. Charles Parish: Des Allemandes Town History." Courtesy of L'Observateur, First published in 'River Current' magazine, January 2000.

Chapter 5
At the Vortex:
Footnotes:

1.) Description of the church services attended by Mrs. Jones and Miss Ferris are taken from Gary D. McElhany, "The Origin and Development of the Mississippi District,"*Heritage Vol. 14 No. 1, Spring1994,* an Assembly of God publication celebrating the fortieth anniversary of the founding of that denomination in Mississippi.

2.) The history of the founding of the Clarendon Assembly of God Church, with Miss Cora Ferris as a charter member, is from *Donley County History, 1879 – 1990 (Curtis Media Corporation, 1931 Market Center Blvd., Dallas, Texas).* From 1940 on the author lived in close proximity to the church and heard the sounds of the "singing from the spirit and speaking in tongues" drifting out of windows of the little pink church building.

3.) Characterization of Cora Ferris' life in Biloxi has been compiled from U.S. City Directories 1821-1989, *Ancestey.com.*, Roy L. Billands, Ocean Springs Archives and Biloxi Historical Society, "Celebrating 75 Years of Ministry," August 20, 1922-1997, Cedar Lake Christian Assembly, Senior Pastor, Ken Broadus and *Assembly of God Heritage, Vol. No. 1 Spring 1994.*

4.) "On High Ground," St. Charles Parish Library, Luling, La.; Lunk, *A Bayou Runs Through It* 78-79.

5.) Robert B. Thomas, *The Old Farmer's Almanac,* (Little. Brown and Company, 1938).

6.) The transcript of the trial, Cause No. 1972, containing the actual confession of Morris Norman, County Attorney R. Y. King's testimony validating the confession and Miss Cora Ferris' testimony regarding the attack, is missing. The story of the attack has been pieced together from the author's familiarity with the setting and from a variety of sources quoting the confession and from other sources describing the appearance, demeanor, typical behaviors of Morris Norman. These include coverage of the story in: *The Donley County Leader, The Clarendon News, The Amarillo Daily News, Amarillo Globe Times, The Houston Post,* letters and statements included in The Classification History of Morris Norman with the Bureau of Classification, Texas Prison System.

7.) "Negro Sought in Clarendon Attack"; "Negro Charged with Assault Will Come to Trial Tues".

8.) "Jailer's Wife Shoots Escaping Prisoner,"; "Obituaries: Pierce."

9.) Southwestern Associated Telephone Company directory, 1938.

10.) "Switchboard 1939," *Flicker.com.* (Picture), *Progress and Changes 1920-30,"How It Works*: When a customer turned the crank on magneto telephone, a drop, showing the caller's number line, fell down just above the caller's line. The operator took any black cord, plugged it into the caller's line, pushed back the front key which was in line with the cord, and said, "number please." She then took the front key which was directly in front of the back cord, plugged it into the called number, and pulled the back key toward her to ring the party's telephone. When the party answered, the connection was complete."; author's memory of a visit to the Southwestern Telephone Company's Clarendon exchange where she observed operator Cordie Thompson manning the switchboard.

11.) "Gun Battle Here Costs Deputy Eye, *The Clarendon News,* January 4, 1934. Mary Jane Hunt, author's grandmother, midwifed his birth in the Wright home east of Clarendon, October 19, 1901.

12.) *"Negro Sought in Clarendon Attack";* "Assault and On Two White Women Here Sunday Night," *The Clarendon News, November 3, 1938; and* "Negro Charged With Assault Will Come to Trial Tues."

13.) The characterization of Texas Ranger Neal Arthur has been re-sourced by 1910, 20, 30 and 40 United States Federal Census; U. S. World War II Army Enlistment Records; U. S. City Directories 1821-1989 – Ancestry.com; Texas Ranger Personnel Records, Texas Rangers Hall of Fame, Waco, Texas; *Amarillo Daily News* articles, his *Houston Chronicle* obituary, March 19, 1995; Louva Hunt, inter-view with Tom Burk, former director Texas Ranger Hall of Fame, September, 2013.

14.) Characterization of Ranger Pat Taliaferro has been resourced by 1910 United States Federal Census, U. S. City Directories, 1821 – 1989; Web: Arizona, Find a Grave Index, 1861-2011 - Ancestry.com; Mike Cox, *Texas Ranger Tales* (Republic of Texas Press, 1997); Texas Ranger Personnel Records, Texas Ranger Hall of Fame, Waco, Texas; newspaper articles from *Amarillo Daily News, Abilene Reporter News, San Antonio Light*; Louva Hunt, interview with Vivian Allen, native of Baylor County, Texas.

15.) Texas Ranger Hall of Fame and Museum, letter to Louva Hunt, August 19, 2013, Utley, *Lone Star Lawmen,* Cecil R. Chesser, *Across The Lonely Years – A History of Jackson County,* (Altus, Oklahoma

Printing *Co.*, 1971); Laur*a* Ferris Sprinkle, *Donley County History, 1899 – 1990.*

16.) Texas Military Forces Museum, e-mail to Louva Hunt, August 20, 2012.

17.) Characterization of Clyde J. Douglas from 1910 United States Federal Census, Texas Birth Index, U. S. World War I Draft Registration Cards – Ancestry.com; "World War I: The Ambulance Services," History of US Army MSC/chapter2.html; Louva Hunt, interview with Mary Douglas, daughter-in-law, March, 2012.

18.) Clarendon Lore to describe the culture of clandestine activities on North Jefferson Street.

19.) A composite of news coverage of the event in *Amarillo Daily News,* October 31, November 1, 3, *The Donley County Leader,* November 3, 1938, *The Clarendon News,* November 3, 1938 and conversations between her parents overheard from the author's window on the adult world.

20.) Ruth Ann Spivey and Rebbeca Chudacoff, interview with Louva Hunt October 2, 2013.

21.) *"Donley Grand Jury Called In Attack Case,"* Morris Norman *Classification History:* Louis Earlix, Headquarters Sixth Corps Area, CCC., letter to Bureau of Classification, November 1, 1938.

22.) Sheriff Guy Pierce, letter to Bureau of Classification, November 14, 1938.

23.) "Donley Grand Jury Called in Attack Case."

24.) Mike *Cox, Texas Ranger Tales; "Negro Sentenced to Die: Convicted Black Is En Route to Death House," Amarillo Daily News,* November 9, 1938.

25.) "Negro Sought in Clarendon Attack;" "Negro Charged With Assault Will Come to Trial Tues."

26.) *"*Donley Grand Jury Called in Attack Case.*"*

27.) *Ibid.*

28.) Roger Estlack, interview with Louva Hunt, 2013, in which Estlack described standard procedures used by reporters.

29.) *"Negro Sought In Clarendon Attack."*

30.) "Charged With Woman Death at Shamrock: Mobs Searched For Five Days," Amarillo *Daily News,* July 16, 1930; *"Attack Case Set Next Week," Amarillo Daily News, November 4, 1938; D*onley County Court Minutes, November 2, A. D., 1938; "Negro Charged With Assault Will Comes To Trial Tues."

31.) Utley, 134-5, 140.

32.) Roger Estlack, interview with Louva Hunt, 2013.

33.) Author's recollections of the event.

34.) "Attack Case Set Next Tues."

35.) Donley County Court Minutes, November 2, 1938·

36.) "Attack Case Set Next Week."

37.) *"Negro Charged In Attack Will Come To Trial Tues,"*

38.) *Ibid.*

39.) *"Attack Case Set Next Week,"* November 3, 1938.

Chapter 6
On Main Street

1.) This chapter was resourced from: Willard Skelton, *A Little Bit of History;* from author's memories of her father's reports of the saga to her mother during the nine days it was taking place in Clarendon collected at the listening post of her window on the world and from the author's experiences of these scenes along Main Street.

Stationed atop her father's high postal clerk's stool, under the command of his duty look and the Postal Rules and Regulations to refrain from setting foot on the floor of the Post Office, she was occasionally allowed to accompany her father during his evening shift in the Post Office. Thus, she witnessed behind the lobby Post Office work routines. These memories were supplemented with interviews with Delbert Robertson, son of Andy Robertson, detailing his memories of accompanying his father as he picked up the mail and delivered it to the train.

Chapter 7
The Cast

1.) "Assault and Indignities on Two Women Here Sunday Night."

2.) Ib*id.*

3.) Characterization of John Deaver is from materials from The John Deaver Collection, Southwest Collection/Special Collections Library at Texas Tech University; John M. Deaver, II, interview with Louva Hunt, January, 2012.

4.)   John M. Deaver II, interview.

5.)   *Ibid*

6.)   *Ibid.*

7.)   Characterization of Judge A. S. Moss is from materials from the John Deaver Collection, Texas Tech Southwest Collection; *Texas State Bar Journal*, December, 1964; John M. Deaver, II, interview; "Address of Nelson Phillips" at the Dinner of the Amarillo Bar Association, December 11th, 1937, for a reflection of the ethical views promoted by the Ethical Committee of the State Bar Association of which Judge Moss held a leadership position.

8.)   Characterization of J. Ralph Porter is from U. S., World War I Draft Registration Cards, 1917-1918 - Ancestry.com; Texas Military Forces Museum, e-mail from lisa.sharik@us.army.mia, August 13, 2012; Dorothy Breedlove, interview with Louva Hunt, 2012; Cindy Burnett, his granddaughter, interview with Louva Hunt, 2012; James R. Lovell, interview with Nita Dyslin, December 6, 2011; "Services Today for J. R. Porter," *Donley County Leader,* October 26, 1956; author's memory of Judge Porter.

9.)   "Funeral Services Held for W. T. Link Sunday," *The Donley County Leader,* September 18, 1969.

10.)   Clarendon Lore.

11.)   Characterization of John Knorpp is from letter from Ann Hommel, February 2, 1979; James R Lovell, interview with Nita Dyslin; "Services Held for Former Civic Leader," *The Clarendon Enterprise,* April 8, 1999.

12.) Jean Stavenhagen, "The Hanging," *Accent West,* June 2010.

13.) "The Press: Old Tack" – Time, Monday July 2, 1951.

14.) Chapter 34, Article 34.04, SPECIAL VENIRE IN CAPITAL CASES:: Texas Code of Criminal Procedure, *Justia US Law.com;* Donley County Minutes, November 2, 1938.

15.) Marquart, 7.

16.) Clarendon Lore concerning rumored Klan activities.

17.) 1930 United States Federal Census, Donley County, author's estimate.

18.) "Action of Jury Meets Approval," *The Donley County Leader,* November 10, 1938.

19.) Roma Khanna, "First Female Juror Paved Way for Women's Rights," *Houston Chronicle,* Sunday, September 26, 2004.

20.) SPECIAL VENIRE, Justia US Law.com.

21.) Donley County Court Minutes, November 8, 1938.

22.) Ibid., November 7, 1938.

23.) Donley County Courthouse Restoration, *Voltz & Associates, Inc.,* Floor plan of Court room as restored, 2004.

24.) Utley, *140.*

Chapter 8
The Trial

1.) "Tuesday, Nov. 8 Is Election Day, *"The Clarendon News"*, *November 3, 1938.*

2.) Donley County Court Minutes, November 8, 1938.

3.) "Negro Is Given Death Penalty On Charge Of Criminal Assault," *Donley County Leader*, November 10, 1938; "Negro Sentenced to Die"; Relevant Criminal Procedures are as found in *Vernon's Texas Statutes, 1936 Centennial Edition* and *1938 Supplement*, Kansas City, Mo. Vernon Law Book Company.

4.) John M. Deaver II, interview.

5.) Classification History: District Attorney's Statement of Offense, John M. Deaver, Donley County, November 13, 1938.

6.) Donley County Court Minutes, November 8, 1938.

7.) "O'Daniel, Wilbert Lee (Pappy)," /The Handbook of Texas Online/ *Texas State Historical Association*, tshaonline.org.

8.) *"Negro Sentenced to Die."*

9.) *Ib*id.

10.) For discussion of Jim Crow thinking of the time, "Marquart, 53, 103, 187; Court House Plan, Second Floor.

11.) Thomas F. Turner, "Prairie Dog Lawyer," *Panhandle-Plains Historical Review*, 1929, II.

12.) "Address of Nelson Phillips," 22.

13.) "John" Knorpp letter.

14.) Classification History: Subject's Version of the Offense, November 9, 1938.

15.) Utley, 152.

16.) *Ibid., 173-4.*

17.) *"Negro Sentenced to Die;" "Negro Is Given Death Penalty On Charge of Criminal Assault," The Donley County Leader, November 10, 1938.*

18.) "Negro Rapist Is Held Here Tuesday," *The Memphis Democrat, November 11, 1938.*

19.) *Ibid.*; Classification History: Subject's Version of the Offense.

20.) Classification History: Earnest Wallace, letter to Bureau of Classification, November 15, 1938.

21.) "Polish Jews Return: Warsaw and Germany Unravel Tangle," "Anthony Eden Resigns," "Hob-Goblin to Radio,"*Amarillo Daily News,* October 31, 1938, "Eleanor in Cincinnati Urges Racial Tolerance," *Amarillo Daily News,* October 19, 1938.

22.) H. G. Wells, 39.

23.) "Negro Is Given Death Penalty On Charge of Criminal Assault."

24.) "Action Of Jury Meets Approval." The 12 members of the jury were: P.L. Dishman, Nolie Simmons, R.C. Bingham, W.R. Morgan. John Naylor, J.W. Bland, Roy Jewell, E.W. Kennedy, Henry Merrick, Frank Howlett, R.E. Clark and C.L. Goin.

25.) *Ibid.*

26.) "College Home Coming Exes To Arrive Tomorrow," *The Donley County Leader*, November 10, 1938.

27.) "Colored Folks of Clarendon Thank Sheriff," *The Clarendon News*, November 10, 1938.

28.) Angela Y. Davis, *Women, Race & Class.* New York: Vintage Books, 1983, 194.

29.) Ed Mannino, "Cruel And Unusual Punishment: Troop v. Dulles (U. S. Law, American History) edmannino.com.

Chapter 9
The Rover - Goin' Home

1.) Characterization of Lizzie Norman, a composite of: 1910, 1920, 1930, 1940 United States Federal Census, Social Security Death Index, 1940 United States Federal Census of Calvert, Texas - Ancestry.com; Robertson County Death Certification; articles from The Hearne Democrat, Newspaper.com; Robertson County Real Property Official Records and materials from Morris Norman Classification History. Characterization of Wesley Norman: a composite of 1880, 1900, 1910, 1920, 1930 and 1940 United States Federal Census, Social Security Death Index - Ancestry.com; Robertson County Death Certificate and materials from Morris Norman Classification History.

2.) J. W. Baker, *A History of* Robertson County, Texas, Sponsored By The Robertson County Historical Foundation), 1970. (Printed by Sherman Books), 438, 9.

3.) Classification History: R. L. Stellbauer, letter to Classification Bureau, November 16, 1938.

4.)   *Ibid.*

5.)   "Justice Acts Speediest As Attacker Dies."

6.)   *Ibid.*

7.)   *Ibid.*

8.)   "Slave Songs Transcend Sorrow, "*Slave Songs – Lyrics and Meaning,* christianity.com.

9.)   *Holy Bible, Revised Standard Version,* Luke: 23: 42.

10.) "Slave Songs Transcend Sorrow."

11.) "There Is a Balm in Gilead - Wikipedia- the free encyclopedia, wiki-pedia.org.

12.) Marquart, *101.*

13.) *Ibid., 26.*

14.) Classification History: List of Correspondence.

15.) Characterization of Morris Norman: A composite of news articles covering his arrest, trial and visit with his family; Classification History.

16.) Classification History: Subject's Version of the Offense, November 9, 1938.

17.) *Ibid.*

18.) Classification History: Lizzie Norman, Family Questionnaire, November 18, 1938.

19.) R.H. Stellbauer letter.

20.) Classification History: "Personality," Classification Summary.

21.) John E. B. Myers, "A Short History of Child Protection in America," (*Family Law Quarterly, Vol. 42, No. 3*, Fall, 2008), 450.

22.) Classification History: Letters of Reference.

23.) *Ibid*.

24.) Ibid; "Action of the Jury Meets Approval."

25.) "Pardon's Board Won't Save Negro From Chair Tonight," *The Donley County Leader,* December 15, 1938.

26.) Paul M. Lucko, "Board of Pardons and Parole," *Handbook of Texas Online,* tshaonline.org. http://www.tshaonline.org/handbook/online/articles/mdbjg

27.) *Ibid*.

28.) Classification History: Mose Dean, letter to Bureau of Classification, November 15, 1938.

29.) Classification History: Letters of Reference.

30.) Classiicaion History: Lorene Stephenson, letter to Bureau of Classification, November 15, 1938.

31.) Classification History: Letters of Reference.

Chapter 10
From Chicago to Clarendon
Footnotes:

1.) Classification History: Madeline L. MacGregor, Executive Secretary, Travelers Aid Society of Chicago, summary of the agency's contact with Morris Norman, November 28th, 1938 in a letter to Miss Ruth Coleman, Chicago Bureau of Public Welfare.

2.) Classification History: Family Questionnaire.

3.) Raymond N. Flynt. "Travelers Aid," socialwelfarehistory.com.

4.) Classification History: John L. Sullivan, Chief of Detectives, to Bureau of Classification, December 21, 1938.

5.) MacGregor letter to Miss Ruth Coleman.

6.) "Humanism," simplypsychology.org.

7.) Classification History: Thomas Lavin of Transportation Services, letter to Miss Ruth Coleman, November 16, 1938.

8.) *Ib*id.

9.) Classification History: Classification Summary.

10.) Author's memory of the Easter Star Rodeo.

11.) John Henry Vaughn, Funeral Information (familyowned.net/obituary) accessed April 21, 2012.

12.) Classification History: Classification Summary.

13.) *Ibid.*

14.) Description of the pimping world on the streets of Chicago in 1938, Iceberg Slim, *Pimp,* (Cash Money Content, 1969, 1987), back cover, 22. 97, 59, 200, 300, 302, 229.

15.) Classification History: Marcno Fisher, State Parole Agent, letter to T. P Sullivan, Division of Supervision of Paroles, Chicago Office, November 30, 1938.

16.) *Ibid.*

17.) Iceberg Slim, *Pimp,* 68.

18.) Classification History: M. E. Gould, letter to Bureau of Classification. (undated)

19.) Classification History: Thomas Lavin, letter to Miss Ruth Coleman.

20.) Classification History: Marcno Fisher, letter to T. P Sullivan, November 30. 1938.

21.) Stan Cohen, *The Tree Army: A Pictorial History Of The Civilian Conservation Corps, 1933-1942:* (Pictorial Histories Publishing Company, Missoula, Montana, 1980), 10.

22.) "CCC Aid Saves Fertile Acres From Erosion," *Rockford Register Republic,* Wednesday, September 23, 1936.

23.) Classification History: Classification Summary.

24.) Harry D. Milne, "Golden Glove Champion," *Rockford Register Republic,* January 16, 1938.

25.) "Donley Grand Jury Called In Attack Case."

26.) "Louis-Schmeling: More than a fight." espn.com.; "Broadcast at Palace," "At The Cave Tonight," *Rockford Register Republic, June 26, 1938.*

27.) Author's memory; for a description of men's clothing, The Complete 1930's Guide, vintagedancer.com.

28.) Classification History: G. J. Sweeney, Supervisor CCC Selection, letter to Mr. Carl J. Martini, June 16, 1938; Morris Norman letter to commanding Officer, Camp Durand, May 14, 1938.

29.) Lorene Stephenson letter.

30.) Classification History: Louis Earlix, Captain, A. G., Res., to Bureau of Classification, November 16, 1938.

31.) Classification History: Classification Summary.

32.) Clarendon Lore.

33.) Iceberg Slim, *Pimp,* "Glossary," 299.

34.) Clarendon City Map.

35.) Clarendon Lore; "Celebrate Golden Anniversary." *Amarillo Daily News,* March 9, 1960.

36.) Clarendon City Map.

37.) "Negro is Held in Clarendon Death," *Pampa Daily News,* April 22, 1936.

38.) "Gun Battle Here Costs Deputy Eye."

39.) Classification History: Guy Pierce, letter to Bureau of Classification, November 14, 1938.

40.) Clarendon Lore.

Chapter 11
The Potter's Hand

1.) Joe Lovell, e-mail message to Louva Hunt, September 29, 2014; "M'Naghten Rules," wikipedia.org.

2.) Chapter 46B, Article 922, Vernon's Texas Statutes, 1936 Centennial Edition (Kansas City, Mo. Vernon Law Book Company).

3.) Marquart, 26.

4.) Carl Basland, Classification in the Texas Prison System," (The University of Texas Publication, No. 3847: December 15, 1938), 10,11.

5.) *Ibid., 13-15.*

6.) Emil Kraeplin, "Psychopathic Personalities," Wikipedia, the free encyclopedia, wikipedia.org.

7.) Basland, 13-15.

8.) Ibid., 15.

9.) Jelain Chubb, State Archivist and Director, Archive & Information Services Division, letter to Chris Stewart, June 10, 2014.

10.) Classification History: Personality.

11.) Classification History: Dr. T. G. Cole, letter to Mr. Bruce W. Bryant, Chairman, Board of Pardons & Paroles, December 5, 1938.

12.) *Vernon's Texas Statutes*, Chapter 46B, Article 922, 1938 Supplement.

13.) *Ib*id.; Basland, 19.

14.) *Vernon's Texas Statutes*, Chapter 46B, Article 922, 1938 Supplement.

15.) Classification History: *Dr.* T. G. Cole, letter to Mr. Bruce W. Bryant.

16.) Basland, 15.

17.) John P. Dworetzky, *Psychology*, (West Publishing Company, St. Paul, 1982), *378*-379; Robert V. Guthrie, *Even the Rat Was White: A Historical View of Psychology Second Edition* (Pearson Education, Inc., 2004), 66-68.

18.) Saul McLeod, Defense Mechanisms. Retrieved from simplypsychology.org/defense-mechanisms.

19.) *Ib*id.

20.) Guthrie, 50-57.

21.) Ibid.

22.) Marquart, 26-28.

23.) *Ibid.*

24.) Guthrie, 90-100.

25.) Marquart, 26-28.

26.)   Ibid.

27.)   Classification History: Personality.

Chapter 12
Explaining Buddy

1.)   Classification History: Description of Convict When Received.

2.)   Classification History: Matt Davis, letter to Bureau of Classification, November 16, 1938.

3.)   Classification History: T. J. Smith, letter to letter to Bureau of Classification, November 16, 1938.

4.)   For an understanding of the impacts that disease, injury, neglect and abuse upon the developing brain of a child have upon their personalities, cognitive functioning and the aberrant behaviors seen in them as adults, this chapter has been guided by Ackerly, S, S. & Benton, A. L. "Report of case of bilateral frontal lobe defect." *Proceedings of the Association for Research in Nervous and Mental Disease 1948." Nervous and Mental Disease Vol. 27 (1948): The frontal lobes (479-504), Baltimore:* Williams & Wilkins Co.; Steven W. Anderson, et al, "Consistency of neuropsychological outcome following damage to prefrontal cortex in the first years of life." *Journal of Clinical And Experimental Neuropsychology 2009, 31 (2), 170-179.;* Paul J.; Eslinger, PhD, et al, "Developmental Consequences of Childhood Frontal Lobe Damage." *Archives of Neurology Vol 49 No. 7, July 1992;* Tiffany W. Chow, MD, "Personality in Frontal Lobe Disorders." *Current Psychiatry Reports 2000, 2:446-451;* Bruce H. Price, et al, "The Compartmental Learning Disabilities Of Early Frontal Lobe Damage, Correspondence to Dr. Bruce Perry," Neurological Unit, Beth Israel Hospital, March

15, 1989; Powell and Voeller, "Prefrontal Executive Function Syndromes in Children," *Journal of Child Neurology* Volume 19, Number 10, October 2004, 792.

5.) *Phineas Gage, Neuroscience's Most Famous Patient,* The Slate Group, a Graham Holdings Company, 2004.

6.) Eslinger.

7.) *Dorothy Otnow Lewis, M. D., Guilty by Reason of Insanity: A Psychiatrist Explores The Minds Of Killers* (Fawcett Columbine: The Ballantine Publishing Group. New York) 1998.

8.) Classification History: List of Correspondence.

9.) Classification History: MacGreagor and Gould letters.

10.) Marquart, 71.

11.) Lewis Adam Liptak, "Court Extends Curbs on the Death Penalty in a Florida Ruling," *The New York Times.* May 24, 2014.

12.) Manny Fernandez and John Schwartz, "Stay of Execution Granted for Texas Inmate, *The New York Times, May 13, 2014.*

13.) Lewis, *Guilty by Reason of Insanity, 251.*

Chapter 13
The Question

1.) Classification History: Stephenson letter.

2.) H. D. Wells 48,78.

3.) "8th Amendment Court Cases, Trop v. Dulles." revolution-war-and-beyond.com/8th-amendment-court-cases.

4.) Classification History: Stephenson letter.

5.) Classification History: Earnest Wallace, letter to Bureau of Classification, November 15, 1938.

6.) "What Are Your Miranda Rights?" MirandaWarning.org

7.) "8th Amendment Court Cases, Furman v. Georgia."

8.) Ibid., "Coker v. Georgia."

9.) Bruce D. Perry and Rennie Pollard, "Altered brain development following global neglect in early childhood," *Society for Neuroscience*: Proceedings from Annual Meeting New Orleans, 1997.

10.) Richard Althouse, Ph.D., "The Genetics of Tribalism and Mass Incarceration: A Conceptual Analysis." *The IACFP Newsletter*, January, 2015.

11.) H. D. Wells, 88.

12.) "8th Amendment Court Cases, Adkins v. Virginia."

13.) "Court Extends Curbs on the Death Penalty in a Florida Ruling."

14.) Kathryn Seifert, Ph.D, "Improved Treatment of Mental Illness Could Prevent Violent Behaviors." *The IACFP Newsletter*, January 2015.

Chapter 14
Mother's There, Expecting Me

1.) Baker, 163.

2.) Baker, *142-154.*

3.) Baker, *464-5.*

4.) 1880 United States Federal Census.

5.) Baker, *282.*

6.) Classification History: Family Questionnaire.

7.) Baker, 280.

8.) Baker, 160-165, 280.

9.) Kristeen Moore, "Whooping Cough (Pertissis)," Healthline. com., July 13, 2012; "Whooping Cough: Causes, Symptoms, and Treatment, webmd.com.

10.) Classification History: Family Questionnaire.

11.) *Ibid.*

12.) Baker, 277, 283.

13.) Classification History: Family Questionnaire.

14.) *Ibid.*

15.) Classification History: JW Doremus, letter to Bureau of Classification, November 14, 1938.

16.) Classification History: Stephenson letter.

17.) "Justice Acts Speediest As Attacker Dies."

18.) Classification History: letter from W. W. Waid, Warden, to the family.

19.) "Clemency Denied for Negro Rapist," *The Abilene Reporter-News.* December 14, 1938.

20.) "The Green Mile, (1999)," –Quotes – IMDb.com.

21.) Baker, 439.

22.) Manny Fernandez, "Texas Prison Burials Are a Gentle Touch in a Punitive System," *The New York Times,* January 4, 2012.

23.) "There is a Balm In Gilead," Slave Songs Transcend Sorrow."

24.) H. G. Wells, *88.*

Chapter 15
Little Weena's Flowers

1.) "Justice Acts Speediest As Attacker Dies."

2.) *Ibid.*

3.) H. G. Wells, 39.

4.) *Ibid.*

5.) Classification History: Gould Questionnaire.

6.) "Negro Charged With Assault Will Come to Trial Tues."

7.) Classification History: Letters from Robertson County citizens.

8.) Wesley Norman - 1910 United States Federal Census; T.J. Smith letter.

9.) Mose Dean letter.

10.) MacGreagor letter.

11.) Lavin letter.

12.) Classification History: Commitment Papers.

13.) *The Green Mile.*

14.) Marquart, 18.

15.) Classification History: Personality.

16.) Dr. Cole letter.

17.) Marquart, 18.

18.) *Ibid.*

19.) "Justice Acts The Speediest As Attacker Dies."

20.) "Two Death Penalty Cases Up to O'Daniel," *Dallas Morning News,* Wednesday, November 23, 1938.

21.) Classification History: Letters to Donley County District Clerk and County Treasure, December 16, 1938.

22.) *The Green Mile.*

23.) Tammy Reynolds, et al, "History of Stigmatizing Names for Intellectual Disabilities Continued," Community Counseling Services, Inc., mentalhealth.net.

24.) Ex Parte Tuttle, 1969, Texas Court of Criminal Appeals Decisions, Texas Case Law. U.S. Law, Justia, justia.com.

25.) Lewis, *Guilty By Reason of Insanity, 251.*

26.) "District court hears pleas in 3 cases," *The Clarendon Enterprise,* November 21, 2013.

27.) H. G. Wells, 92.

28.) "Negro Executed For Attack," *The Houston Post,* December 16, 1938.

29.) Iceberg Slim, 59.

30.) "They Crucified My Lord," Slave Songs.

Chapter 16
Epilogue

1.) "Avoidance," *PTSD: National Center for PTSD ptsd.va.gov.*

2.) Ann Hommel letter.

3.) Naoma Rippetoe, interview with Louva Hunt, 2013; "Obituaries: Rippetoe," *The Clarendon Enterprise,* April 2, 2014.

4.)   Donnie Hall, Interview with Louva Hunt, 2013.

5.)   "Justice Acts The Speediest As Attacker Dies."

6.)   The account of the James Monroe Ferris family and the early years of Cora and Mattie have been resourced by: "Navajoe, Oklahoma," Wikipedia.org.; Texas Ranger Hall of Fame and Museum, letter to Louva Hunt, August 19, 2013; J.M. Ferris, Texas Ranger Enlistment; Utley, *Lone Star Lawmen*, 223-252; Chesser, *Across The Lonely Years; Rufus Buck Gang: The History of Organized Bands of Bank and Train Robbers Who Terrorized The Prairie Towns of Missouri, Kansas, Indian Territory and Oklahoma for Half a Century*, Bramhall House, New York, 1964; Laura Ferris Sprinkle, *Donley County History*.

7.)   For characterization of Cora Ferris' life in Biloxi (see chap. 5, ns, 3,4); Roy L. Billande, "Brother Isaiah: References: 'Brother Isaiah Arrives,' *The Daily Herald,* June10, 1922, 'Brother Isaiah, En Route to Biloxi,' *The Jackson County Times*, August 30. 1922."

8.)   Lunk, *A Bayou Runs Through It* (see chap. 4, n. 1).

9.)   *Across the Lonely Years*; "T. Jones Passes On Following Paralysis," *The Clarendon News*, September 17, 1933.

10.) "Pierce."

11.) John M. Deaver, II, interview; letter to Louva Hunt, April 14, 2016.

12.) Arthur Neal (see chap, 5, n. 13).

13.) Taliaferro (see chap. 5, n. 14).

14.) "Services Held for Former Civic Leader."

15.) "Obituary: Hauser" *Galveston Daily News.* June 3, 1997.

16.) *State Bar Journal, December 1964.*

17.) "Services Today for J. R. Porter".

18.) "Services Held For C. L. Goin," *The Donley County Leader, July 8, 1954.*

19.) "Last Rites for Jessie Walter Green Held Here Monday," *The Donley County Leader, November 14, 1965;* "Funeral Services For W. T. Link Held Sunday.

20.) Spivey interview and e-mail.

21.) Account of Lorene Stephenson family history resourced by: 1940 United States Federa Census, Ancestry.com; e-mail from Barbara Kievit-Mason, Sam Houston State Teachers College, June 10, 2013; "Foster - Stephenson," *The Hearne Democrat*, Fri, January 5, 1840; Hughes Tool Company," "Brown Shipbuilding," Wikipedia – the free encyclopedia. wikipedia.org; Weldon Stephenson Death Certificate, August 4, 1943; Carl Foster, United States Federal Census, Social Security Death Index, 1935-2014, November 30, 1989, – Ancestry.com ; Lorene Stephenson Foster – OBIT, December 13, 1998, Family History & Genealogy Message Board – Ancestry.com; Author's visit to Nesbitt-Beck Prairie Cemetery.

22.) Account of the Norman family resourced by: Wesley Norman, Death Certificate, December 13, 1946, 1880 through 1940 United States Federal Census data, deed records Calvert, Texas, Death Certificate, Harry Norman, June 8, 1956, "Andrews Fire Sweeps

Home: Child Killed," *The Odessa American*, Fri., May 20, 1960; Fletcher Norman, Death Certificate, December 10, 1971; Lizzie Norman, Death Certificate, March 10, 1984.

23.) "Goin Home," lyrics.astraweb.com.

Sources
Books

J. W. Baker, *A History of Robertson County, Texas*, Sponsored by The Robertson County Historical Foundation (Printed by Sherman books, 1970).

Carl Basland, *Classification In The Texas Prison System* (The University of Texas Publication, No. 3847, December 15, 1938).

Cecil R. Chesser, *Across the Lonely Years – A History of Jackson County* (Altus, Oklahoma Printing Co., 1971).

Stan Cohen, *The Tree Army: A Pictorial History Of The Civilian Conservation Corps, 1933-1942* (Pictorial Histories Publishing Company. Missoula, Montana, 1980).

Mike Cox, *Texas Ranger Tales: Stories That Needed Telling* (Republic of Texas Press, 1997).

Angela Y. Davis, *Women, Race & Class* (New York: Vintage Books, 1983).

Donley County History, 1879-1990 (Curtis Media Corporation, 1931 Market Center Blvd.

John P. Dworetzky, *Psychology, Second Edition* (West Publishing Company, St. Paul 1982).

Robert V. Guthrie, *Even the Rat Was White: A Historical View of Psychology Second Edition* (Pearson Education, Inc., 2004).

Dorothy Otnow Lewis, M. D., *Guilty By Reason Of Insanity: A Psychiatrist Explores The Minds Of Killers* (Fawcett Columbine The Ballantine Publishing Group New York, 1998).

Ray Lunk, *Des Allemandes: A Bayou Runs Through It* (Lulu Enterprises, Inc., Raleigh, N. C., 2011).

James W. Marquart, Sheldon Ekland-Olson, Jonathan R. Sorenson, *The Rope, the Chair, & the Needle: Capital Punishment in Texas, 1923-1990* (University of Texas Press, Austin, 1994).

Sara R. Massey, ed., *Black Cowboys of Texas* (Texas A&M University Press, 2000).

Iceberg Slim, *Pimp,* (Cash Money Content, 1969, 1987).

Robert M. Utley, *Lone Star Lawman: The Second Century Of The Texas Ranger,* (Oxford University Press, 2007).

H. G. Wells, *The Time Machine* (The Random House Publishing Group, 1968),

Newspapers

NEWSPAPERS HAVE BEEN ORGANIZED IN THE ORDER THEY WERE CITED.

1.) "Services Held for Ham McCampbell," *The Donley County Leader,* October 2, 1966.

2.) "KGNC: The Globe News Radio Station," *Amarillo Sunday Globe-News*, October 30, 1938.

3.) Benjamin Keck, "October 30 Memorable Night in 1938." *Amarillo Daily News*, October 30, 1978.

4.) "Rulers Of The Home To Present Their Royal Tom Thumb Wedding," *The Donley County Leader*, November 3, 1938.

5.) "Negro Charged With Assault Will Come to Trial Tues.," *The Donley County Leader*, November 3, 1938.

6.) "Justice Acts Speediest as Attacker Dies," *The Amarillo Globe*, December 16, 1938.

7.) "Negro Sought in Clarendon Attack," *Amarillo Daily News*, Monday Morning, October 31,1938.

8.) "A Million Imaginations Afire As Radio Realism Shakes The Nation," Amarillo Daily News, October 31, 1938.

9.) "Donley Grand Jury Is Called in Attack Case," Amarillo Daily News, October 31, 1938.

10.) "Thousands Witness Parade of the Ku Klux Klan in Clarendon Last Thursday Evening," *The Clarendon News*, June 15, 1922.

11.) "To The Lovers of Law and Order," *The Clarendon News*, August 3, 1922.

12.) "Veteran Officer Added to Highway Patrol Forces Here," *Amarillo Globe-News*, September 29, 1938.

13.) "Youth Confesses Robbery of Bank," *San Antonio Light*, November 12, 1936.

14.) "Plainview Murder Suspect Slain: Shot Down in Lockney Barn" *Abilene Reporter News*, May 31, 1939.

15.) "Timeless Tales: Jailer's wife shoots escaping prisoner," *Amarillo-Globe News*, September 30, 1999.

16.) "Obituaries: Pierce," *The Clarendon Enterprise*, October 26, 2000.

17.) "Woman Jailer Plays Big Part In Negro Hunt, "*The Donley County Leader*, November 3, 1938.

18.) "Gun Battle Here Costs Deputy Eye," *The Clarendon News*, January 4, 1934.

19.) "Attack Victim Pleads For Peaceful Trial," *Wichita Daily Times*, November 4, 1938. HERE?

20.) "Assault and Indignities on Two Women Here Saturday Night," *The Clarendon News*, November 3, 1938.

21.) "Arthur," *Houston Chronicle*, March 19, 1995.

22.) "Negro Sentenced to Die: Convicted Black Is En Route to Death House." *Amarillo Daily News*, Wednesday Morning, November 9, 1938.

23.) "Charged With Woman Death At Shamrock: Mobs Searched For Five Days,"*Amarillo Daily News*, July 16, 1930.

24.) "15 Minutes Is Required For Jury Decision," *Amarillo Daily News*, July 28, 1930.

25.) "Attack Case Set Next Tuesday," *Amarillo Daily News*, November 4, 1938.

26.) "Services Today For J. R. Porter," *The Donley County Leader*, October 26, 1956.

27.) "Services Held For W. T. Link Sunday," *The Donley County Leader*, September 18, 1969.

28.) "Services held for former civic leader," *The Clarendon Enterprise.* April 8, 1999.

29.) "Action of Jury Meets Approval," *Donley County Leader*, November 10, 1938.

30.) Roma Khanna, "First Female Paved Way For Women's Rights," *Houston Chronicle*, Sunday, September 26, 2004.

31.) "Tuesday, Nov. 8 Is Election Day," *The Clarendon News*, November 3, 1938.

32.) "Negro Is Given Death Penalty On Charge of Criminal Assault, "*The Donley County Leader*, November 10, 1938.

33.) "Negro Rapist Is Held Here Tuesday," *The Memphis Democrat*, November 11, 1938.

34.) "Clarendon College Home Coming "Exes" To Arrive Tomorrow," *The Donley County Leader*, November 10, 1938.

35.) "Negro Must Die On Dec. 16," clipping taken from John M. Deaver Collection, Texas Tech Southwestern Collection, citation data missing.

36.) "Colored Folks of Clarendon Thank Sheriff," *The Clarendon News*, November 10, 1938.

37.) "Pardon's Board Won't Save Negro From Chair Tonight: Crime Most Heinous In Annals Of Panhandle Criminal History, *"The Donley County Leader*, December 15, 1938.

38.) "Celebrate Golden Anniversary, *"The Amarillo Daily News*. March 9, 1960.

39.) "Negro is Held in Clarendon Death," *Pampa Daily News*, April 22, 1935.

40.) Adam Liptak, "Court Extends Curbs on the Death Penalty in a Florida Ruling," *The New York Times*, May 27, 2014.

41.) Manny Fernandez and John Schwartz, "Stay of Execution Granted for Texas Inmate," *The New York Times*. May 13, 2014.

42.) "Clemency Denied For Negro Rapist," *The Abilene Reporter-News*, Wednesday, December 14, 1938.

43.) Manny Fernandez, "Texas Funerals Are a Gentle Touch in a Punitive System," *The New York Times,* January 4, 2012.

44.) "Death Cases Await Daniel Term," Austin, November 22, *INS*

45.) "District court hears pleas in 3 local cases," *The Clarendon Enterprise*, November 21, 2013.

46.) ."Obituaries: Rippetoe," *The Clarendon Enterprise*, April 2, 2014.

47.) "T. Jones Passes on Following Paralysis, "*The Clarendon News,* September 17, 1933.

48.) "Obituary: Hauser," *Galveston Daily News,* June 3, 1991

49.) "Services Held For C. L. Goin," *The Donley County Leader,"* July 8, 1954.

50.) "Last Rites For Jessie Walter Green Held Here Monday," *The Donley County Leader,* November 14, 1965.

51.) "Andrews Fire Sweeps Home; Child Killed, "*The Odessa American,* Fri, May 20, 1960.